SODA AND FIZZY DRINKS

Edible

Series Editor: Andrew F. Smith

EDIBLE is a revolutionary series of books dedicated to food and drink that explores the rich history of cuisine. Each book reveals the global history and culture of one type of food or beverage.

Already published

Apple Erika Janik, *Avocado* Jeff Miller, *Banana* Lorna Piatti-Farnell, *Barbecue* Jonathan Deutsch and Megan J. Elias, *Beans* Nathalie Rachel Morris, *Beef* Lorna Piatti-Farnell, *Beer* Gavin D. Smith, *Berries* Heather Arndt Anderson, *Biscuits and Cookies* Anastasia Edwards, *Brandy* Becky Sue Epstein, *Bread* William Rubel, *Cabbage* Meg Muckenhoupt, *Cake* Nicola Humble, *Caviar* Nichola Fletcher, *Champagne* Becky Sue Epstein, *Cheese* Andrew Dalby, *Chillies* Heather Arndt Anderson, *Chocolate* Sarah Moss and Alexander Badenoch, *Cocktails* Joseph M. Carlin, *Coffee* Jonathan Morris, *Corn* Michael Owen Jones, *Curry* Colleen Taylor Sen, *Dates* Nawal Nasrallah, *Doughnut* Heather Delancey Hunwick, *Dumplings* Barbara Gallani, *Edible Flowers* Constance L. Kirker and Mary Newman, *Edible Insects* Gina Louise Hunter, *Eggs* Diane Toops, *Fats* Michelle Phillipov, *Figs* David C. Sutton, *Foie Gras* Norman Kolpas, *Game* Paula Young Lee, *Gin* Lesley Jacobs Solmonson, *Hamburger* Andrew F. Smith, *Herbs* Gary Allen, *Herring* Kathy Hunt, *Honey* Lucy M. Long, *Hot Dog* Bruce Kraig, *Hummus* Harriet Nussbaum, *Ice Cream* Laura B. Weiss, *Jam, Jelly and Marmalade* Sarah B. Hood, *Lamb* Brian Yarvin, *Lemon* Toby Sonneman, *Lobster* Elisabeth Townsend, *Melon* Sylvia Lovegren, *Milk* Hannah Velten, *Moonshine* Kevin R. Kosar, *Mushroom* Cynthia D. Bertelsen, *Mustard* Demet Güzey, *Nuts* Ken Albala, *Offal* Nina Edwards, *Olive* Fabrizia Lanza, *Onions and Garlic* Martha Jay, *Oranges* Clarissa Hyman, *Oyster* Carolyn Tillie, *Pancake* Ken Albala, *Pasta and Noodles* Kantha Shelke, *Pickles* Jan Davison, *Pie* Janet Clarkson, *Pineapple* Kaori O'Connor, *Pizza* Carol Helstosky, *Pomegranate* Damien Stone, *Pork* Katharine M. Rogers, *Potato* Andrew F. Smith, *Pudding* Jeri Quinzio, *Rice* Renee Marton, *Rum* Richard Foss, *Saffron* Ramin Ganeshram, *Salad* Judith Weinraub, *Salmon* Nicolaas Mink, *Sandwich* Bee Wilson, *Sauces* Maryann Tebben, *Sausage* Gary Allen, *Seaweed* Kaori O'Connor, *Shrimp* Yvette Florio Lane, *Soda and Fizzy Drinks* Judith Levin, *Soup* Janet Clarkson, *Spices* Fred Czarra, *Sugar* Andrew F. Smith, *Sweets and Candy* Laura Mason, *Tea* Helen Saberi, *Tequila* Ian Williams, *Tomato* Clarissa Hyman, *Truffle* Zachary Nowak, *Vanilla* Rosa Abreu-Runkel, *Vodka* Patricia Herlihy, *Water* Ian Miller, *Whiskey* Kevin R. Kosar, *Wine* Marc Millon, *Yoghurt* June Hersh

Soda and Fizzy Drinks

Drinks

A Global History

Judith Levin

REAKTION BOOKS

For Emily Flanagan and Nicole Flanagan

Published by Reaktion Books Ltd
Unit 32, Waterside
44–48 Wharf Road
London N1 7UX, UK
www.reaktionbooks.co.uk

First published 2021

Printed and bound in India by Replika Press Pvt. Ltd

A catalogue record for this book is available from the British Library

ISBN 978 1 78914 491 8

Contents

Introduction 7

1 On the Way to Fizzy Drinks 15

2 Health and Pleasure: Soda Fountains 39

3 Around the World in a Soda Bottle 61

4 Big Soda 79

5 The War(s) Against Soda 97

6 Plus ça Change 117

Recipes 143

References 157

Select Bibliography 164

Websites and Associations 168

Acknowledgements 170

Photo Acknowledgements 172

Index 174

Introduction

The fizzy drinks of my 1960s suburban New York childhood were Dr. Brown's Cel-Ray, chocolate egg creams, ginger ale and quinine water. Cel-Ray is celery-flavoured fizzy water and reliably appears on 'weirdest-sodas-ever' lists. It is what New York Jews traditionally drink with pastrami sandwiches. Chocolate egg creams – containing flavoured syrup, milk and soda water, but neither egg nor cream – are another New York regional speciality, drunk most often at soda fountains. Ginger ale was medicinal: it settled the stomach. Quinine water was what the grown-ups mixed with gin, rather as British colonials had drunk it to fend off malaria when posted abroad. And my mother told a story of when she was a child, and her father used to squirt her and her brother across the breakfast table with the seltzer siphon. As Americans living in the northeast (but not in Boston), we called most of these drinks *soda*. Unflavoured fizzy water was 'seltzer'. 'Tonic' meant quinine water. There were also 'Fizzies', a brand of sweetened, flavoured tablets that created a temporarily effervescent drink when mixed with water. I didn't have sweet drinks often. My parents believed sugar to be unhealthy.

These drinks serve to introduce much of what I will write about in this book: soda comes from fountains, bottles and

Pastrami sandwich with Dr. Brown's Cel-Ray soda, Traditions Eatery, Lawrence, New York.

siphons – and occasionally from fizzing tablets. Soda is medicinal. Soda is sugary. Soda is global (lemon and ginger were among the first fizzy flavours to travel the earth) but also local. Dr. Brown's Cel-Ray Soda was originally Dr. Brown's Celery *Tonic*. Available by 1868, it was one of the first health tonics to become a branded fizzy drink. It was also a

...shionable flavour: celery was new to America, and there were multiple brands of celery soda. For those of us who grew up with it, the celery tang complements the salty, fatty taste of pastrami. Thus, like other flavours we learn and love in childhood, the taste of sweet drinks becomes a part of who we are – as individuals, as members of a family or as ethnic, regional or religious groups. Soda is full of memories, as well as full of sugar; in some ways it becomes part of our lives and seems to belong to us, although in other ways it belongs to those who produce and sell it.

This book looks at how and why carbonated drinks became so popular around the world, and how they have changed over time and in different places.

For a beverage made of water, fizz and something sweet, fizzy drinks have provoked a lot of arguments: they are the most innocent of little pleasures, or a leading cause of health problems; they are medicinal tonics, or dangerously addictive drugs. Carbonated drinks were not invented in the United States, yet fizzy drinks in general, and Coca-Cola in particular, have been perceived as American.

The arguments about fizzy drinks began with what to call the stuff. In the food and beverage industry, they are *carbonates*, or CSD (carbonated soft drinks). Yet in the United States alone there is so much variation in the generic term for sweet fizzy drinks that it has been the subject of a scholarly article, regional linguistic surveys and a map that periodically goes viral.[1] It is 'soda', a name left over from when it contained bicarbonate of soda. It is 'pop', for the sound the bubbles make or the sound of a bottle being opened. In parts of New England it is 'tonic', from a time when the drink was medicinal. In some regions of the United States – and some countries – the generic word is 'Coke', because when soda first arrived on the market, Coca-Cola was the first or the most visible.

In the UK, and sometimes Australia and New Zealand, th[...] generic term is often 'fizzy drinks', but in Britain and the U.S. a hundred years ago, and in parts of South America today, the drink was sometimes called 'champagne', for its bubbles. It can be 'minerals' in Ireland, or 'lemonade'; 'lolly water' in Australia or *Sifon* in Romanian. Cool drinks. Cold drinks. Sweet drinks.

Thus, even what the drink is called reveals something of its history and ingredients, of the sound it makes and how it feels in the mouth. For years in my family the generic term was 'tingly', because that's what my first granddaughter called it.

That characteristic tingle-in-the-mouth quality is not universally experienced as a good thing. Fizz – and the practical questions of how to get the fizz into the water and the fizzy water distributed to customers – drove the beginning of the industry. Carbonation was a goal, and people were not dissuaded from that goal, even when the results blew up, literally: the early history of soda is punctuated by news reports concerning exploding bottles and fountains and the obituaries

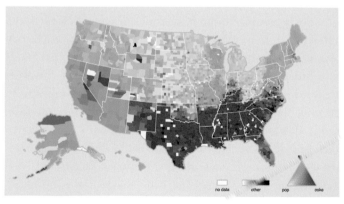

What do you call the fizzy stuff? Versions of a U.S. 'Pop vs. Soda' map have appeared (and sometimes gone viral online) since the first one was produced by a linguistics survey in 1996.

. people killed by them. Carbonation has traditionally been undesirable in, for example, the Far East. There, it is perceived as strange and even painful. And the consumption of iced drinks has not always been considered a good idea. Traditional Chinese medicine says that consuming iced drinks is dangerous, and until about 150 years ago many American and European medical authorities agreed. Some people still do. So people in East Asia drink soda, but its acceptance resembles that of cheese in Japan: something culturally odd and unpleasant (cheese is, after all, milk long past its sell-by date) that became popular with people who wanted to be modern or who liked sweets, and Japanese carbonated drinks are generally less fizzy than drinks from elsewhere. Some young Chinese friends, for instance, sometimes tell me that 'sizzling' drinks hurt the tongue and they'd rather drink sour plum juice to cool off – or tea. When the American writer William Tappan Thompson drank soda water for the first time in 1845, he didn't enjoy the experience either. The carbonated water tasted like 'a pint of frozen soapsuds' and his 'tongue felt like it was full of needles'.[2]

The fizzy sweet stuff is now a worldwide, multinational industry worth hundreds of billions of dollars a year. There are global brands and regional ones, drinks that (theoretically) taste the same anywhere in the world, and drinks – some of them owned by the same corporations – that are created for specific countries and tastes. Most of the world doesn't drink celery-flavoured soda or Russia's tarragon-flavoured soda. And when, in 2009, Hindu nationalists in India announced the development of a medicinal soda made from cow urine, the matter was widely reported. The fizzy drinks of one culture are a matter of curiosity to people elsewhere.

As potables go, fizzy drinks are frivolous. They are cheap – but not so cheap that everyone can have them. One man who came to the United States as a child, a refugee after the Second World War, was surprised and charmed that in America food *made noise*. He had never had fizzy drinks or breakfast cereal before, and sixty years later still spoke with wonder at his memories of the sparkling exuberance of carbonation and fizz and popping sounds, of foods doing things that are not necessary. Many of us live in a world of consumer goods that do a lot more than is necessary. We're sated – hence the ever-widening diversity of drink flavours, packaging and advertising. And we might not even recognize that we respond to the sound or colour of our drinks.

The people who invented and sold mineral waters, artificially aerated waters and then flavoured carbonated drinks had no electricity or reliable clean water or ice. They did, however, have customers who were becoming 'consumers'. It is the creation of modern consumers and a global economy, as well as sweet drinks themselves, that is saturating the world. 'Coca-colonization' preceded 'McDonaldization' as a concern. Some of the encounters between local tastes or values and international ones are to do with flavour; others with political associations. As for the former, sometimes people simply want flavours that are familiar to them: malt-flavoured beverages are popular in Germany, the Caribbean and Africa; Iranians and Afghans like yoghurt-flavoured fizzy drinks. The Frenchman behind Mecca Cola, however, created a product for people who liked the taste of cola, but disliked America's foreign policy in the Middle East.

As sweet carbonated drinks have spread across the world, the same issues have arisen again and again: how should they taste? What should or shouldn't be in them? In what ways are they good or bad (medicinally, morally, culturally, nutritionally)? What is their place in the local food culture? In what ways are fizzy drinks (as a category of beverage) and any given

Interior of a seltzer factory, illustration from Louis Figuier, *Les merveilles de l'industrie* (The Marvels of Science, 1873–7). From left to right: filling siphons and bottles; putting siphons in a wooden box; carrying out a box; and sealing a bottle.

fizzy drink in particular defined by their *context*? 'Context' includes flavours, containers and advertising campaigns; the history of a drink's arrival in a place; claims about the liquid's qualities; product names; and the places and events where soda is consumed. It includes associations created by marketing, as well as personal memories created by individuals and families. All of these contribute to what the drinks *mean*. The meaning of drinks is a subject that interests researchers and historians of food, and also those involved in concocting drinks or planning marketing campaigns. Most recently it has interested neuroscientists, who can identify the parts of the brain that 'light up' on an MRI when people are eating or drinking something they like the taste of, and who can also see the different parts of the brain that light up when people are consuming something with which they have emotional connections. Thus branding, which involves expectations, memories and associations, changes the way we experience a food or drink The results of the MRIS prove what historians and researchers of food and drink have long known: we experience the same tastes in different ways based on what we think and feel. All foods are embedded in culture; certainly for carbonated sweet drinks, their symbolic meanings are far more complex than the water, gas and sugar that form their corporeal substance.

I

On the Way to Fizzy Drinks

Fizzy drinks have many beginnings and many histories.

They began with naturally occurring mineral waters that bubbled up from the ground, and the belief in their curative properties, and then in the efforts of chemists to replicate them and pharmacists and others to dispense them. The first fizzy water 'flavours' included Spa, Pyrmont, Vichy, Ballston and Selter (that is, seltzer), named for the places where the natural springs were found.

Fizzy drinks also begin as part of the larger category of soft drinks, as distinguished from hard, or alcoholic, drinks. These soft drinks are sometimes cold and sweet, and people like the taste of different ones in different places. Throughout their history, carbonated sweet drinks competed with other local drinks, existed alongside them and were perhaps influenced by their taste.

Soda pop, in the United States, arose out of the nineteenth-century tradition of patent medicines that promised miracle cures and personal transformation, and whose advertisements changed promotional campaigns forever. In England and Scotland, too, some fizzy drinks originated in tonics and medicinal drinks. Flavoured fizzy water was also used by pharmacists to hide the taste of bitter medicines.

Ironically, then, sweet carbonated drinks originate in three traditions that were supposed to be healthful.

Sparkling Waters

Before 'soda fountain' meant a place to buy a fizzy drink, or the machinery that dispensed it, it meant a place where naturally occurring mineral waters bubbled up from the earth. The ancient Romans called the springs *aqua saltare*, or dancing water, and believed in the benefits of bathing in these waters at such places as Vichy and Pyrmont, France; Nieder-Selters, Germany; and the city of *Aquae Sulis* – later called Bath, England. By the sixteenth century, the waters were drunk as well as bathed in, and Spa, Belgium, had given its name to the historic treatments associated with the mineral benefits of the springs. In the American colonies, too, springs in such places as Ballston in Saratoga, New York, had in the past attracted the attention of native peoples, and then that of the doctors and philosophers of the colonizing Europeans. Thomas Jefferson and George Washington were among those interested in the possible curative value of mineral waters.

Soaking in hot water eases a variety of aches, and a change of diet and routine may have made people feel better, but the curative powers of drinking the waters did not, in truth, extend to the cure of 'kidney stones, scrofula, salt rheum, erysipelas, dyspepsia, general disability, chronic consumption, catarrh, bronchitis, constipation, tumours, piles and cancerous affections', as claimed by one bottler of mineral waters in the years following the American Civil War. On the other hand, when Dr Frederick Slare presented his analysis of Pyrmont Waters to the Royal Society of London in 1717 he noted that these waters were *chalybeate*: that is, they contained iron, and

Jan Luyken, *Bathhouse in Aachen*, 1682, engraving. Aachen, Germany, has been a spa city known for its sulphurous water since Roman times. Modern advertisements still vaunt the water's healing effect on such conditions as osteoporosis, gout and degenerative diseases.

were 'indicated in all diseases which are caused by anaemic composition of the blood'.[1] Indeed.

Scientists and entrepreneurs were fascinated by waters that tasted good or at least seemed to cure disease even if they tasted bad. Even though – to a limited extent – the natural waters could be bottled, the bottled waters tended to lose their fizz, and shipping them was expensive. The researchers wanted to understand the nature of the fizz in order to duplicate it. Motives ranged from scientific curiosity – what *was* that fizz, anyway? – to wanting, altruistically, to make the water cures available to people who could not afford to go to the springs, to wanting to make money by supplying water to customers. Thus the search for artificial fizzy mineral waters embodied many of the strands of the later industry: the product is a medicine, a source of pleasure, a series of technological problems – and a cash cow.

Although the British scientist, clergyman and political theorist Joseph Priestley is frequently credited with being the

Two early attempts at keeping the fizz in the fizzy water: J. Ladd's ginger beer bottle, produced in Adelaide, South Australia (*right*), and the Hamilton (torpedo) bottle from J. Schweppe & Co, London (*below*), which had to lie on its side to prevent the cork from drying out.

first to put fizz into still water, in the 1770s, he was building on the work of scientists before him. In 1620 the Flemish chemist Jan Baptista van Helmont coined the word 'gas'; the gas of sparkling waters was identified as carbon dioxide only in 1792. Yet even without the knowledge of the gas's chemistry, scientists were able to extract it from chalk or limestone and to understand that it was different from 'common air'. In the 1750s Joseph Black called it 'fixed air' and recognized it as the gas produced by fermentation. David McBride, an Irish surgeon, identified it – hopefully, though incorrectly – as an antiscorbutic: something that would prevent or reverse scurvy, long a concern of explorers and navies.

Travelling to the brewery near his home in Leeds, Priestley recognized the 'fixed air' fizzing above the vats of fermenting beer. By quickly pouring still water back and forth from one glass container to another above the vats, he created a mild effervescence as the water absorbed the gas. He later created this gas by combining sulphuric acid and chalk in a bottle, thereby creating carbon dioxide, and capturing it in a pig's bladder. Priestley then transferred it into an inverted, water-filled bottle and shook this container until the water had

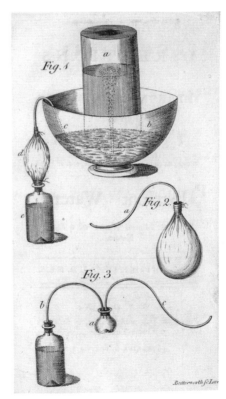

Joseph Priestley's first apparatus for 'impregnating water with fixed air'. Fig. 2 is the bladder of an animal.

Nooth's apparatus (*left*); seltzogene for homemade soda water, late 19th century, British Syphon Company, London (*right*). The wire mesh is for safety.

absorbed the gas. Priestley's *Directions for Impregnating Water with Fixed Air* (1772) received the highest honour awarded by England's Royal Society – ironically, for his work in creating an antiscorbutic. Both the Royal Society and Priestley had made a false connection between the slightly acidic bright quality of the water and the acid of lemons and limes, fruits long recognized as antiscorbutics.

By 1774 Dr John Nooth had copied Priestley's method but made the apparatus entirely of glass. No more animal bladders. A slightly improved version of Nooth's device was marketed, and by 1777 more than a thousand had been sold to people living as far away as the East Indies. Under the name 'gasogene' or 'seltzogene', versions of this device were used for home carbonation into the twentieth century. Even Sherlock Holmes

…d one. Additionally, using Nooth's apparatus, merchants began to sell artificial Seltzer and Pyrmont waters. One such merchant was Thomas Henry, who sold the waters at his apothecary shop in Manchester, England.

However, it is Jacob Schweppe who is most responsible for launching artificial fizzy waters.[2] The German-born master jeweller was living in Geneva when he read Priestley's work on the carbonation of water and built a copy of Priestley's device. Disappointed by the quality of the carbonated water it produced, he began to tinker with it. He also built a machine, based on a suggestion of Priestley's, that used a 'condensing engine', a pressure pump which caused more gas to be absorbed by the water, and then improved upon that. Schweppe moved to London in 1792 to produce and sell aerated water of a quality that was superior to anything on the market. Nonetheless, he struggled with his competitors, business partners and

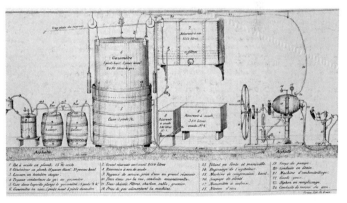

Jacob Schweppe's drawing of his Geneva System apparatus, 1783. The container at the far left begins the process of agitating chalk and sulphuric acid to produce carbon dioxide, which is then cleaned by being passed through barrels of water into the biggest container, called a gasometer. A pump forces the gas into a barrel where it is dissolved in water. The soda water tank is the one directly under the water tank, to the right of the gasometer

One of a series of paintings by Maynard Brown for Schweppes
advertising, c. 1900. The Royal Warrant of Appointment stamp is
embossed in the lower-right corner, which also says 'Royal Table Waters'.

distribution. Only when he was close to giving up did he receive the endorsements of British scientists and physicians that would lead to his becoming the most profitable supplier of artificial mineral waters in London. Many of the achievements of the Schweppes company came after the business was sold in 1798. It was in the early years of the nineteenth century that Schweppes products were exported throughout the British Empire and the company became the mineral water supplier to Britain's upper class and royalty.

Soft Drinks

The directions in which soda and soda flavourings were initially taken – and the drinks they largely replaced – were dictated by the various liquids that people around the world already drank. Wherever fizzy drinks travelled, local drink flavours were generally adapted to become fizzy-drink flavours.

People drank water, but water, aside from mineral waters, was the drink of the poor, of those with no other options. The royal patent in 1236 to pipe water from Tyburn to London provided water for 'the poor to drink and for the rich to dress [cook] their meat'.[3] Fresh water at that time might not have been an option because it was unavailable, especially in cities or on shipboard, because it was considered unhealthy (due to contamination or people believing cold drinks were dangerous) or because it was boring.

By the eighteenth century, the drinking habits of the Americans and the British had been changed by the adoption of new drinks: tea, coffee and chocolate. Historian John Burnett identifies a 'hot drinks revolution' in the seventeenth century, when the newly imported beverages began to replace the porter that many – Samuel Pepys, for one – drank at breakfast.[4] Their arrival coincides with the introduction of cheap cane sugar imported by the West India Company, so that these somewhat bitter drinks could be consumed *sweetened*, as they had not been in their countries of origin. They also introduced consumers to caffeine.

Early non-alcoholic drinks that preceded and were, in part, replaced by coffee, chocolate and tea, and then later by sodas, included those made and consumed in or near people's homes: infusions made with herbs and plants, 'small' (low-alcohol) beers and ales made from brewing herbs and plants, fruit juices, watered fruit juices, barley water, liquorice water and any number of milk or milk-based drinks, some of them

Drinks were sold at stalls, carts or from a tank on the seller's back: the illustration here depicts a liquorice-water seller in Paris, drawn by Jean Geoffroy for *Harper's Young People* (1890).

fermented. Cordials were syrupy reductions of fruit and sugar, sometimes preserved with alcohol. Later the 'cordial' came to mean a sweet liqueur and, in Britain, 'squash': a fruit-flavoured concentrate to be diluted with still or sparkling water.

The fact that some of the earliest and most popular carbonated drinks were ginger beer and root beer reminds us that the boundary between alcoholic and non-alcoholic beverages was not absolute. Early soft(ish) drinks included the small

Soft drink stands could be plain or fancy: seen here are a seltzer-water cart in Berlin, illustration from *Harper's Weekly*, 14 August 1875 (*above*), and spruce-beer sellers in Jamaica, illustration published in *Harper's New Monthly Magazine*, January 1861.

beers that working people in Britain and America made at home or received as part of their pay. These flavourful drinks contained fizz that resulted from the brewing process rather than from the deliberate addition of gas. Food historian J. C. Drummond estimates that a seventeenth-century English boy might have drunk three pints a day of small beer, which would provide him with 500–600 calories, and was 'a good, sound, healthful drink'.[5] German children drank *kinderbier* (children's beer). Small beers and root beers – including those made from dandelion and burdock, horehound, ginger, nettle, sarsaparilla, parsnip and sassafras – contained less than 2 per cent alcohol.

By the early to mid-nineteenth century in London, home-brewed beers and ales were no longer drinks that the English poor and industrial workers could enjoy at home. Malt and other materials needed for brewing were taxed; people who worked in factories had neither the time, money nor ingredients to brew. The English poor turned to tea – often heavily sweetened tea – incurring the wrath of those who saw tea drinking as a waste of money or an aping of their social betters. Diets at this time were so impoverished, however, that hot tea might have been the only thing people were 'cooking'. Accompanied by cheap bread, these drinks were brewed from the cheapest and most adulterated teas on the market or – especially in the country – infusions of mint, sage, chamomile, blackcurrant leaves, sassafras root, ginger, or other herbs or spices. They were less 'tea' than boiling water poured over herbs, and then sweetened. People became accustomed to drinking sugar-sweetened liquids.[6]

Nineteenth-century American cookbooks list a variety of cooling drinks, not always making a distinction between those that fizzed and those that didn't – commonly featured together were lemonade (not typically a fizzy drink in America); a 'cream nectar', frothed with egg whites and the combination of tartaric acid and (baking or bicarbonate of) soda, which tasted of sugar and 'essence of wintergreen or any other flavouring'; and cold tea.

Eighteenth- and nineteenth-century Americans farmers, sweating in the fields, also drank small beers, or 'switchel' (also called haymaker's punch), prepared from water, ginger, vinegar and molasses or maple syrup. Contemporary medical opinion said that while it was dangerous to drink something very cold while sweating, the 'hot' quality of the ginger and the sharpness of vinegar cooled the body without danger. These drinks also replenished what we now identify as electrolytes. So-called 'shrubs' were made of water, vinegar and fruit juice. The acid of the vinegar was refreshing; it also functioned as a preservative if these drinks were 'put up' (preserved for storage).

The word 'shrub' comes to American English by way of the Arabic *shariba*, 'to drink', as do many of the words used to describe soft drinks and their ingredients, including 'sherbet,' 'julep' and 'syrup'. Because Muslims are prohibited from drinking alcohol, their culinary traditions include numerous drinks made from the syrups of fruits, flowers and herbs. Called 'sherbets' in British English, they impressed the Europeans, who encountered them as early as the sixteenth century. In 1627 in London Francis Bacon imbibed sherbets 'made in Turkie of lemons, roses, and violets perfumed'.

'Sherbet' came to mean the powders to make fizzy drinks (in Britain), as well as the sweet dipping powder for lollipops; in the United States, it is a frozen dessert (sorbet, but with dairy). At least until the mid-1900s, the children of Istanbul could buy sherbets of lemon, tamarind, pomegranate or orange from a man with a brass tank on his back.[7]

The Arabic influence popularized sweet drinks in Renaissance Europe. By the sixteenth century, wealthy Italians drank

Sherbet seller in Istanbul, *c.* 1920.

lemonade. By 1676 sellers of lemonade (and other drinks) in Paris, or *limonadiers*, had established themselves as the Companie des Limondiers. The well off could drink lemonade at Le Café Procope; others could buy it in the street, dispensed from a tank. The popularity of the *limonadier* and his wares is responsible for one of the modern French words for a soft-drink seller, and *limonade* becomes a generic term for soft drinks of any flavour, as well as giving rise to the *-ade* suffix of the English lemon-, orange- and raspberryade.[8]

Patent Medicines

The nineteenth century was a time of urbanization and commercialization, of industrialization and of mass immigration from Europe to the United States. There was a greater demand for non-alcoholic drinks than there had been in the past, as the temperance movement gained strength in Britain, the United States and parts of Europe – alongside a greater demand for (dubious) remedies, health tonics and patent medicines, some of which had existed for centuries.

These 'medicines' were among the first commercial products to have trademarks and brands. Until the nineteenth century, most ordinary products didn't even have packaging. The shopkeeper scooped your oatmeal or flour out of a barrel. Its quality was guaranteed (or not) by the trustworthiness of the shopkeeper. Some versions of a product were superior to others – pure white flour and white sugar were superior to brown, for example – but this was reflected in the price.

Patent medicines, however, did not fulfil a need in quite the same way as flour or sugar; a need had to be created, and since buyers could distinguish one nostrum from another only by their names and bottles, the sellers of patent medicines began a tradition of wild claims and carnivalesque advertising. Because the ingredients themselves were so inexpensive, the sellers of these substances could spend a great deal of their profits on advertising – the first high-budget ad campaigns in history.

Patent medicines, herbal medicines and tonics offered hope at a time when medical doctors had little to offer. The medicines might have worked because the herbs were effective – for example, ginger is effective at settling the stomach. They might have worked because the herbs were in a base of alcohol or opiates. Or from the placebo effect. Or not at all.

The other benefit on offer was the promise of self-transformation in a country dedicated to the possibility of self-transformation. Sellers claimed that the purchase and consumption of their product would change your life. The appeal was of magic, of fascinating ingredients from distant lands, of the native lore of Indigenous Americans, of secret recipes. One generic name for the elixirs was 'snake oil', because many claimed that as an ingredient. The sellers of these nostrums used celebrity endorsements; 'before' and 'after' images; and promises of renewed youth and beauty, glamour, wealth, energy and happiness.

Recitations of the claims of Victorian-era medicine shows and patent medicines are always good for a laugh. By

Label for Bursas, a soft drink by Thomas & Evans, South Wales, made from burdock, dandelion and sarsaparilla, and marketed as a 'health drink'.

and large, we don't really believe that there is a pill that will cure all possible maladies. However, we periodically *do* long to be happier, healthier and wealthier, to throw away whatever we're bored by and to experience the exotic. We want relief from pain of various kinds – physical, emotional, financial, social, spiritual. Furthermore, the claims made by producers of modern 'functional' soft drinks rival those of the Victorian era.

Sugared fizzy water is not necessary to our diets. It might taste good, but it is empty beyond its promises; the snake oil of consumables: it will not change your life. The popularity of one brand over another is not always even based on taste: in blind taste tests, consumers not only reliably fail to distinguish their favourite cola from any other, but they sometimes fail to distinguish cola from ginger ale. A history of soda is, in part, the history of what these drinks come to mean to people. How and why do people choose one set of meanings over another? Do they reject traditional drinks and embrace new ones? Do they accept what is unfamiliar or adapt it to what they already know and like?

Soft Drinks in London, 1851: A Snapshot

In the days before mass media, one way people learned about new products was from international exhibitions. London's Great Exhibition in 1851 was the first of these fairs to take advantage of the new British railroads. In its six-month run, more than 6 million people visited the Crystal Palace, including nearly one-third of the population of Britain.

At the Great Exhibition, the Schweppes company paid £5,500 (£537,000 today; u.s.$767,388) for the privilege of

The famous crystal fountain at the Great Exhibition in 1851, where the Schweppes company sold their waters.

supplying fair-goers with aerated lemonade and a variety of mineral waters. The Schweppes company gained considerable attention from its presence at the Crystal Palace, selling over a million bottles at the Exhibition alone. The image of the Exhibition's dazzling, iconic 8-metre-high (27 ft) crystal fountain, commissioned by the Schweppes company, still appears on the Schweppes logo.

Already in 1851 there were numerous manufacturers of bottled cordials, as well as different mineral waters. These included Robinson's Patent Barley Water, Hooper's Sarsaparilla, syrups from Crosse & Blackwell and Soyer's Orange Citron Lemonade and Nectar.

Alexis Soyer, a Frenchman who moved to London in the early 1800s, resembled a modern celebrity chef more than one would believe possible. He published cookbooks, developed his own line of cookware and opened a culinary theme park across the road from the Great Exhibition. In 1848 he began selling a blue fizzy drink called Soyer's Nectar. ('Nectars' vaguely related to his version appeared for many years in soda-fountain manuals.) The inflated prose of his advertisements gives us a flavour of the time, if not of the drink:

> Imagine the juices of the most delicious fruits mingled
> with the scientific dash of a master-hand – the racchar-

The crystal fountain appears on the Schweppes company's logo to this day.

ine tartness of the raspberry, the mellower flavour of the apple, a suspicion of quince, and idea of lemon – and all creaming up in a state of effervescence. That is Soyer's Nectar![9]

Also, he said, it could cure feverish pain and giddiness.

Downmarket from Soyer and Schweppes at the Crystal Palace were the street sellers of what we would now call soft drinks. The journalist Henry Mayhew investigated the street sale of various drinks, which he sometimes called 'pop', tracing sales of ginger beer back to about 1822. Vendors told him that their customers are 'chiefly those who have "a penny to spare", rather than those who have "a penny to dine upon"', at a time when a penny bought a piece of fried fish and a piece of bread.[10]

Some of the sellers of ginger beer brewed and bottled daily for the 'good quality', penny-a-bottle trade, using a pound of ginger, lemon acid, the essence of cloves, yeast and a pound of raw sugar for 11 l (3 gallons) of water. The sellers were, however, experiencing competition from the new fountains, most of them hired from ginger-beer manufacturers, which produced a 'ginger beer' – the quotation marks are Mayhew's – of water, lemon juice (called 'lime', because lime was fancier), sugar and oil of vitriol (sulphuric acid). This was carbonated with gas rather than brewed, and 'the harder you pumps, the frothier it comes', said one of the fountain men. 'The fountains will destroy all the fair ginger-beer trade,' predicted an ex-ginger-beer brewer. Ginger beer was also sold in bottles from stalls that were adorned with brightly coloured pictures (when chromolithography was a new technology): one example showed a woman in gorgeous robes serving a frothing ginger beer to a showily dressed gentleman.

'Mush fakers' and ginger beer makers, photograph by John Thomson
published in Adolphe Smith, *Street Life in London* (1877). A 'mush faker'
repaired and sold umbrellas.

Some street lemonade was made to order from a fizzing
acid and alkali mixture (which might or might not have
included lemon), but, like the ginger beer, lemonade might
have also been bottled, either by the street seller or a drinks
company. It too might have been dispensed from a fountain

– the handsomest fountain Mayhew saw was made fro:
mahogany, looked rather like an upright piano on wheels anc
was drawn by two ponies.

'Persian sherbet' was like lemonade, except that it was less
sour; the luridly blue nectar (à la Soyer) contained more sugar
than lemonade and was flavoured with exotic spices such as
cinnamon.

Some of the sellers advertised their wares: 'Iced lemonade
here! Iced raspberryade, as cold as ice, ha'penny a glass, only
a ha'penny!' One seller insisted that lemonade-drinkers are a
'more respectabler class [than ginger-beer drinkers]', and that
boys sometimes ordered the exotic drinks because 'the colour
and the fine names attracts them'.

Thus Mayhew describes sellers advertising their wares in
ways that elevated and misrepresented the drinks, in order
to make them more desirable. They modified their product
so that poorer people could afford it. Sellers decried one
another's tricks while defending their own. (They argued
about ingredients, about froth, about what we might now call
'truth in advertising'.) They quarrelled about the distinction
between buyers of ginger beer and those of the 'more respectabler' lemonade: drinks confer status, even those bought for
a penny or a half-penny. Sellers worried that factory products
were replacing homemade products. The drinks that accompanied fast food were sold to people who had neither the
time nor the money to make their own. In all these ways, the
scenes Mayhew described sound very modern.

Wealthier patrons of non-alcoholic drinks were home or
at their clubs with their gasogenes, or bought bottled water
from Schweppes. By the mid-nineteenth century, there were
more than fifty soft-drinks manufacturers in Britain, and bottled water was available from 36 English spas and imported
from abroad.[11] Middle-class ladies might drink homemade

lemonade, barley water or toast water, and water their wine or sherry.

And yet, in 1888, one Englishwoman said plaintively, 'If some genius would invent something cheap, healthy, palatable and without alcohol in it, I for one will patronize him widely and give him honourable mention.'[12] There seemed to her too little novelty among available drinks.

The state of non-alcoholic potables in America was far more varied, in part because of the soda fountain.

Soda fountain in Miller and Shoemaker's Corner Pharmacy, Junction City, Kansas, 1899.

2

Health and Pleasure: Soda Fountains

The earliest makers and bottlers of fizzy drinks were European, but soda in the United States blossomed because of the soda fountain – a phrase which referred both to the apparatus used to create and flavour the artificial waters *and* to some of the places serving them. And because of the elaboration of the apparatus, the places, and the drinks themselves, which were unconstrained by the technical issues of preserving the drinks for bottling, fizzy drinks went wild in the United States.

The oft-cited connection between pharmacies and carbonated mineral waters began as something straightforward. The compounding of the artificial waters was an exacting matter requiring skills most likely to be found among chemists and pharmacists. In the early 1800s, pharmacists had to be able to make the pills and other medicines they sold, so they had the ability and equipment to crush and weigh the minute amounts of mineral salts needed to concoct mineral waters that imitated those of the famous spas. Some of the waters were themselves seen as medicinal, although they were also being drunk as table waters or mixed with liquor. Also, these sweetened or flavoured liquids masked the taste of foul-tasting drugs.

During the first decade of the eighteenth century, multiple pharmacists in Philadelphia sold carbonated water, and at least one of them flavoured it: in 1807, pharmacist Townsend Speakman sold something called 'Nephite Julep', a combination of fruit juices and soda water. 'Nephritic syndrome' was kidney disease; 'julep', in British English, was a sugary syrup produced to mix with medicines. This is one example of soda's pharmaceutical connections. And yet, drinking mineral water in the morning was a fashionable activity: its medical uses and its social uses are tightly connected from early on in its history.

If one were looking for a time and a place to begin soda-fountain history, one might try Manhattan during the summer of 1809, which found itself with four competing mineral water fountains.

Benjamin Silliman travelled to Europe in 1805 to collect the books and lab equipment he would need for his work in Yale University's chemistry department in New Haven, Connecticut. Already a fan of mineral waters from his experiences taking the waters in Saratoga, New York, he returned to New Haven with one of Nooth's carbonating machines and successfully bottled and sold some soda water. He soon ran into a problem, however, after building a larger carbonating machine. 'I cannot procure any glass bottles that will not burst, nor any stone ones which are impervious to the fixed air,' he wrote to a friend. (The supply of reusable bottles from abroad was limited even before the u.s. government passed a law restricting the import of foreign bottles.) When the demand for his product exceeded his bottle supply, he moved his apparatus to a pharmacy in New Haven, and then to a separate shop. By the summer of 1809, he and a couple of business partners had added a fountain to New York City's elegant men-only Tontine Coffee House in the business district, and opened their own shop at the City Hotel. Their competition came from the pharmacist Joseph Hawkins, who had been selling mineral waters in Philadelphia, and a New Yorker, the Irish-born artificial-mineral-water seller George Usher. That Usher's business was the most successful offers an instructive lesson in the sale of fizzy water. His establishment was the most fashionable and the most elegant. He kept his waters colder and fizzier than competing products, welcomed custom from women as well as men, stayed open on Sundays and supplied his patrons with free newspapers and novels. His shop was next to a park so that people could take little strolls and then return. More than any of his competitors, he envisioned a place where customers could enjoy their drinks, socialize and – to use an anachronistic term – 'hang out'. 'Style, I find, has many devout worshippers,' he explained.[1]

The competition in New York that summer laid out the future path of the soda fountain and precipitated the spread of soda fountains across the United States, as well.

Francis Guy, *Tontine Coffee House*, NYC, *c.* 1797, oil on linen. The Tontine is the building on the left with the flag on its roof.

Soda fountains became associated with American pharmacies because of mineral water's early status as medicine. Although soda water – with or without the bicarbonate of soda for which it was named – was dropped from the u.s. Pharmacopeia, the official annual compilation of drug information, in 1831, by that time the soda fountain was already becomng a fixture in pharmacies, as well as in cafés, candy stores and, ultimately, establishments called soda fountains or ice cream parlours. Eventually, soda fountains also became common in '5 and 10 cent stores', such as Woolworth's, and in department stores.

Historians of fizzy drinks commonly write of them as a medicine that became a treat, but the distinction was never that clear. 'Taking the waters' at a spa had long been as much a matter of fashion as of health, and both pharmacists and soda-fountain operators combined liquids, flavours, sugar and sometimes remedies into glasses.

The flavouring of carbonated waters in America developed steadily but without a lot of documentation. Rather than finding patents or announcements, we simply find descriptions of people drinking it and writing about it. One of the earliest mentions is in an 1807 English advertisement for 'aerated lemonade'.[2] In 1812 the English poet Robert Southey described eating supper at an inn where he 'drank some most admirable cyder, and a new manufactury of a nectar, between soda-water and ginger-beer, and called pop, because "pop goes the cork" when it is drawn, and pop you would go off too, if you drank too much of it.' Another Englishman, Frederick Marryat, described the booths along Broadway in New York City selling 'porter, ale, cider, mead, brandy, wine, ginger-beer, pop, soda-water, whisky, rum, punch, gin slings, cocktails, mint juleps, besides many other compounds, to name which nothing but the luxuriance of American English could invent a word' on 4 July, Independence Day, 1837.[3] By the time a man named William J. Jenks was serving his apprenticeship at a pharmacy in Philadelphia between 1837 and 1845, his description of their syrups as 'made from fruit by expression in a hand press' was merely an assertion of the high quality of their wares. He took fruit flavouring for granted.

The technology used by the early pharmacies and soda fountains had somewhat advanced from Nooth's apparatus, but not by much, and the technological challenges were great. An acid and a carbonate had to be combined and the resulting carbon dioxide dissolved in water. But when the carbon dioxide was compressed into a tank, before being mixed with the water, it would explode if the pressure got too high (and make not-very-fizzy water if it was too low). The water also had to be filtered, but there was no knowledge of germs in the early nineteenth century, so there was a certain amount of guess work or knowledge and experience required in deciding when the water was clean. Dispensers learned – eventually – not to use materials such as copper or lead that would leach poison into the water. The product also had to be chilled, at a time when the only ice available was harvested in the winter and stored until the following summer. This was not only because cold fizzy water was more desirable but because colder water better absorbs the gas.

Above ground, a pipe (perhaps hidden by a wooden column or something more elaborate) rose through the counter. A semicircular pipe called a gooseneck – because of its resemblance to one – dispensed the water with the turn of a spigot into a bottle (not a glass), which was held firmly against the spigot lest the water spray everyone in the vicinity.

There were, however, technological advances. In England, John Matthews had used powdered calcium carbonate (whiting) or chalk to mix with sulphuric acid, but when he moved to New York in 1821, he discovered that marble was more readily available. He bought up all the scrap marble from New York City's new St Patrick's Cathedral, which was under construction on Fifth Avenue. That was enough marble for about 25 million gallons of effervescent water. Matthews employed a man named Ben Austen, who had been enslaved in North Carolina, and the two of them worked out that Austen was able to measure the pressure on tanks of carbon dioxide with his thumb: he would hold his thumb over a small opening in the side of the tank for as long as possible, and when he couldn't keep his thumb steady, the pressure was correct – approximately 10 bars (1034214 Pa, or 150 psi). (Fifty years later, 'thumb measure' was still a rude term in the soda business for doing things inexactly.) Over the years, Matthews invented – or hired people who could invent – such things as a gauge to measure the pressure of the gas and safer, non-reactive linings for soda-water tanks. He would eventually become known as 'the father' (or 'king' or 'Neptune') of soda water: his contributions were a combination of technological improvements, thinking big and understanding his market.

In 1854 Gustavus Dows, working in his brother's pharmacy in a mill town outside of Boston, became tired of shaving ice to put in drink and invented and patented a mechanical ice shaver, as well as a draft arm that allowed the carbonated water to be dispensed directly into a glass of syrup rather than having to be drawn into a bottle and then mixed. Soda fountains were becoming more elaborate, as well as technically more complex. Dows eventually created a fountain encased in marble with silver-plated spigots, and opened his own establishment in Boston. He began serving his flavoured

James W. Tufts's 'Cottage' model soda fountain.

sodas with shaved ice, 'as fine as snowflakes', and added cream. It was called 'ice cream soda' (although Dows meant something closer to iced-cream soda), and it was a hit.

At the Exposition Universelle in Paris in 1867, Dows operated an American restaurant (which failed because the French disliked American food) and a soda fountain that was an enormous success. Paris newspapers reported that *soude américain à la crème glacée* (American soda with frozen cream) sold as many as 4,000 glasses each day. *Harper's New Monthly Magazine* translated a comment from a Paris newspaper: 'It is really one of the curiosities of the Exposition to watch the

Victor Rose, 'Exposition Universelle de 1878 – Médaille d'or', engraving in *Le Monde illustré*, 1 February 1879. International fairs and exhibitions introduced people, whether able to attend in person or not, to things new or foreign.

representatives of every nation on the face of the globe as they make a first trial of the new beverage. The crowd is so great that they are formed into a line by the police.'[4] A report to the U.S. Senate notes that 'soda like theirs was unknown in France, and I believe Europe till these gentlemen introduced it. It was an *American specialty* . . . It was popular with the mass of the people, and even kings and emperors often partook of the delicious draught.'[5]

There were soda fountains in Europe before the 1867 Exposition Universelle. Called *buvettes à eaux gazeuses* (carbonated water kiosks) in France and *Trinkhallen* (refreshment

John Matthews has been called 'The Father of the Soda Fountain'.
The three upper central taps are artificial mineral waters: Vichy,
Seltsers and Geyser. The larger spigots on either side are plain fizzy
water. The bottom row are syrups, including lemon, ginger, sarsaparilla,
chocolate, vanilla, cream, pineapple, coffee and nectar.

kiosk) in Germany, they supplied 'temperance' drinks – plain
seltzer water, or seltzer flavoured with currant or orange syrup,
or sometimes ginger beer or lemonade. Rather than generat-
ing their own gas, these booths have been supplied by portable
fountains or from gasogenes. None of these – not even the
excellent products of Schweppes – sound like the ones that
Dows served. What Dows and the other American soda
fountains sold was meant to *delight*.

The Paris newspaper, as well as the report to the Senate, both suggested that soda was American because it appealed to people from all walks of life. This is a theme that occurs again and again, and is one part of the explanation for how a European and British product became defined as quintessentially American. Frederick Marryat, reporting on the profusion and variety of drinks available in New York City in 1837, had offered another: there were so many drinks that 'nothing but the luxuriance of American English could invent a word' for them all. The drinks were democratic, diverse and slightly over-the-top. I guess that's a reasonable description of America.

In the 1870s, as the United States was recovering from the Civil War, many, if not most, American towns and cities had soda fountains, and each locale vied with one another to have the most beautiful and expensive fountain, as well as the largest. The largest a *Harper's Weekly* writer had seen in the 1890s, in New York City, could draw 32 kinds of syrup and eight kinds of artificial mineral water. 'This monster requires eighty gallons of syrup to fill all its cans and has 250 feet [76 m] of conducting and cooling pipe.'[6]

The fountains of the period had become increasingly elaborate. In 1868 John Matthews published three catalogues of soda-fountain equipment, which included his machinery for making and dispensing carbon dioxide, the technical part of making soda water. It also included an extensive variety of soda fountains, the equipment that mixed in the syrups and dispensed the drinks, differentiated less by anything technical than by how big and fancy they were – although the large ones could hold more flavours of syrup than the small ones. He recommended a small one, the $188 'Jack Frost', for towns of fewer than five hundred people. The 'Frost King', on the other hand, cost $2,976. It was made of polished marble that

had been engraved, gilded, burnished and bejewelled with
'60 real stones'.[7] Additionally, in the same catalogues, he listed
elaborate glassware, decorative spoons and fancy serving
dishes. Even the glass containers to hold drinking straws were
decorative. Soda fountains, as places, were intended to appeal
to all the senses.

James W. Tufts and Charles Lippincott paid $50,000 for the exclusive
right to sell soda water drinks at the 1876 Centennial Exhibition in
Philadelphia, Pennsylvania – and to show off the largest soda water
apparatus in the world. It was made of marble and had 28 soda and
mineral water tubes and 76 syrup dispensers.

For the Centennial Exhibition in Philadelphia in 1876, two of Matthews's competitors, James Tufts and Charles Lippincott, paid $50,000 for the right to sell soda. Tufts designed a fountain that was 10 m (33 ft) high and had 104 spigots that dispensed mineral waters, plain water and syrups. It was the largest fountain in the world. Soda fountains – like the international exhibitions themselves – were about fantasy and ingenuity, yet the exhibitions were also where entrepreneurs and ordinary citizens encountered new technology, new styles and new wants.

As the soda fountains became more elaborate, so did their offerings, both in number and in complexity. Early nineteenth-century flavours – in addition to those based on the taste of waters from various mineral springs – had included vanilla, chocolate, ginger, lemon, a few other fruit flavours and some flavours people would have recognized from home-made drinks, such as root beer, sarsaparilla and birch beer. But more exotic flavours and combinations – as well as fancy and evocative names – soon became part of the selling of soda, and the experience of drinking it, and pharmacists and soda-fountain operators wanted to mix their own flavours. Even when proprietary drinks – the ones whose names we know and which will be discussed later – became available, pharmacists advised one another to stay away from the named brands. 'Do not display them more than is necessary,' one pharmacist advised. 'It is easier and more profitable to concoct your own drink than to sell somebody's [*sic*] else.'[8] By the late 1800s, one flavour list included – in addition to its more than 25 fruit flavours – almond, anise, celery, champagne cider, cinnamon, cognac, coffee, coriander, cream soda, egg phosphate, grenadine, horehound, maple, mead, mint julep, mocha, nutmeg, orris root, peppermint, pistachio, raspberry vinegar, rose, violet, walnut cream and wintergreen.

Soda-fountain drinks weren't limited to a mere fifty or sixty syrup flavours. The making of a good soda involved more than mixing sweet flavoured syrup and fizz. By combining syrups, adding raw eggs (there were special techniques for mixing in eggs), liquors (a lot of soda-fountain drinks included liquor), foaming agents and other ingredients, pharmacists and soda-fountain clerks could offer hundreds of drinks. Drinks with added cream were a whole category unto themselves. After 1867 one favourite additive was acid phosphate, which was newly available commercially. The phosphate lent the drinks a sourness, an acid bite, yet did not add a flavour, as lemon or lime would – in the way that cane sugar is a pure sweetness without flavour. Phosphate also contributed a slight saltiness, thereby enhancing the soda's other flavours and amplifying the slightly sour and acid taste of the carbon dioxide itself.[9] Soda is sweet, but like all sweet things, it is less interesting if it is *only* sweet, hence the addition of an acid. Moreover, in a soda fountain the size and number of bubbles could also be adjusted, affecting how the drink felt in one's mouth.

Soda bottlers, discussed in the next chapter, will have fewer options; later, people making sodas with artificial sweeteners will have to compensate for the loss of sugar in the 'mouthfeel' of the drinks. 'Mouthfeel' is a modern, technical term used in the food and drinks industries but its meaning is reasonably straightforward: for a drink, it refers to the thinness or thickness of the liquid, to its viscosity, and to how long the flavour stays in the mouth and lingers afterward.

Trade journals – such as *Pharmaceutical Era* or *The Soda Fountain* – helped small-town soda-fountain owners to address American customers' desire for novelty and glamour, as well as teaching them the fine points of mixing different drinks. Drink ingredients became part of niche marketing, as did drink names and locations, and the appearance of the fountains themselves. In the years before phosphate mineral salts became a fizzy-drink flavouring ingredient, phosphoric acid was a pharmacist's remedy, prescribed as a 'general tonic, aphrodisiac and stimulant of the nervous and cardiovascular systems'. The drinks that contained phosphoric acid, eggs or bitter ingredients such as quinine were understood to be *men's* drinks. Cream or chocolate sodas were feminine. Drinks were graced with fanciful names: Persian Sherbet, Ambrosia Frappe, Bowler's Favorite, Hyde Park Tally-Ho. The novelties had to keep up with the times: in the early 1900s, with the invention of the first affordable automobiles and America's love affair with them, there was a drink called 'Auto Smash' that consisted of bloody-looking strawberry and grape syrup over shaved ice.[10] Some specialities were regional: pink-coloured New Orleans cream nectar, which tasted of almond and vanilla; or coffee soda (favoured largely by Italians) and celery soda (favoured mostly by Jews) in New York City. Ice cream, whipped cream, fruit, and fruit- or flower-flavoured syrups were just some of the ingredients that could be added to a soda.

Soda fountains also sold 'hot sodas', which could either be hot water with sweet syrup, or hot chocolate, tea or coffee. Even bullion found its way onto hot soda lists, as people running soda fountains struggled to make soda-selling profitable all year round.

The enormous range of flavours available might be a tip-off that some of these fizzy drinks were artificially flavoured. In several of the classic reference books of recipes for pharmacists or owners of soda fountains – Albert Ethelbert Ebert's *Standard Formulary* (1896) and William S. Adkins's *Practical Soda Fountain Guide* (1911), for example – the writers describe the care that must be taken in preparing fresh-fruit syrups. Ebert's recipe for strawberry syrup calls for fresh ripe strawberries and sugar, which are layered and left for several hours to express the juice, which is then boiled, strained and bottled for, he says, that day's use. Adkins describes making cream syrup from a quart of fresh cream, a pint of fresh milk and sugar. In *The Standard Manual of Soda and Other Beverages* (1897), A. Emil Hiss provides recipes for everything from clam broth to kefir, including a recipe for a beverage to serve to those customers who, when asked what flavour they want, answered: 'Don't care'. Hiss notes that any flavours can be used for this, including whatever isn't selling well, but then suggests a combination of pineapple syrup, strawberry syrup, vanilla extract and port wine. Even the preparation of a 'Don't Care' was exacting. Other trade journals provided their own recipes, and 'Don't Care' regularly appeared on soda-fountain machines among the other labelled flavours.

A small soda fountain might make a few flavours from scratch, but many used fruit extracts (real fruit essences preserved in alcohol) or artificial flavours, a book of which was published by 1860. Thus there were multiple ways to create, for example, pineapple-flavoured soda – one of which involved no pineapples. (It was made of chloroform, aldehyde, ethyl butyrate, amyl butyrate, glycerine and sugar.[11]) Fountain operators could buy dozens of flavours of 'artificial fruit essences'. Englishmen James Mew and John Ashton, in their comprehensive book *Drinks of the World*, in 1892, were disgusted to learn of these. They warned their readers, 'Beware . . . of one compound ether, which gives the taste of cinnamon, and is, Ethyl Perchlorate. This mixture is *explosive!!!*'[12]

Soda fountains were almost always more than a place to drink a soda. They embodied the spirit of fun that the French noticed when Dows served them ice-y cream soda and the exuberance (and absurdity) of the overwrought soda-fountain machines that Matthews and his competitors designed. Anne Cooper Funderburg, author of an especially fine history of the American soda fountain, complains that those machines looked like they were designed by 'art school dropouts'. She does, however, admit that they embodied the aesthetics of the time.[13] American Victorians never saw a decoration, flourish, fancy or useless add-on that they didn't like. In their soda fountains – as in their architecture and homeware – they were aiming for bling. They revelled in the ornamentation and elaboration made possible by industrialization.

Quite apart from tasting what was in the glass, going to have a soda included the experience of being in the places anchored by these grand machines and decorated in the same aethetic. Both the drinks and the places were novel and exciting – and the sodas were relatively inexpensive, even if the machinery was not. A hundred or more years later, soda advertisements would show someone drinking a soda, surrounded with friends or family and sunshine. They often show celebrities enjoying the drinks, inviting the consumer to identify the product with those people. There is a common style of advertisement in which someone uses a product and is instantly transported from a mundane location – an office, a kitchen – to a Caribbean beach, a cruise ship or someplace else one would wish to post on social media. But the grand soda fountains of the nineteenth century did this literally: people who lived ordinary lives *did* go someplace glamorous. Matthews's 1868 'Frost King' fountain could be attached to gas pipes for illumination at night at a time when most Americans still lit their houses with kerosene lamps, but even the simpler fountain shops were a contrast with what 'real life' looked like for most people.

Examples of the old-fashioned soda fountains still exist today, one of them in Columbus, Indiana. It was started in 1900 as a Greek immigrant family's sweet shop. At the 1904 World's Fair in St Louis, Missouri, the Zaharakos brothers saw onyx soda fountains made by a new-ish company called Liquid Carbonic (which, by selling tanks of liquefied carbonic acid, had made maintaining soda-fountain equipment much easier). They bought two. They also bought a fancy Tiffany-style lamp (that doubles as a soda-water dispenser), and a few years later, an elaborate German-made Orchestrion (rather like a player piano, except that it sounds like a whole orchestra).[14]

This was not an especially fancy soda fountain for the period. Most of the customers weren't wealthy. The owners lived in modest quarters above the shop. But soda fountains like theirs immersed customers in an environment that appealed to all the senses: everything was shiny, bright and sparkling; they provided good tastes, but also good smells,

The Liquid Carbonic Co. exhibited their equipment and served drinks at the 1904 World's Fair in St Louis, Missouri.

The Zaharakos brothers bought two of the fountains and a Tiffany-style lamp/soda water dispenser, which they then installed in their soda fountain in Columbus, Indiana, shown here in 1915 and 2016.

music and physical comfort. Additionally, they were examples of what the American urban sociologist Ray Oldenburg calls 'third places': the first place is home; the second, work; and the third is a place of voluntary, informal gatherings – a café in Paris, a piazza in Italy, the English pub. Or, in the u.s., the soda fountain.[15]

In 1920 the United States passed a constitutional amendment making it illegal to produce, transport, buy or sell alcoholic beverages. Fizzy drinks and the places that served them had some new customers during the Prohibition era. 'The bar is dead, the fountain lives, and soda is king!' crowed the trade journal *Drug Topics*.[16] Those fountain operators who hadn't served a large male clientele before learned or invented 'manly' drinks, which might have included cayenne pepper, or even whiskey, since drugstores were the only places allowed to sell alcohol (for medicinal purposes, of course). During Prohibition (1920–33), as during the nineteenth-century temperance

St Louis-based beer maker Anheuser-Busch switched to non-intoxicating and legal 'near beer' during Prohibition with Bevo, marketed as a 'soft drink'.

movement, fizzy drinks grew in popularity. Additionally, flavoured fizzy drinks had a new role – to hide the taste of bootleg liquor – and their use as 'mixers' popularized 'dry' ginger ale, as opposed to the older, sweeter, heavier ginger ales, and gave Americans a taste for fizzy mixed alcoholic drinks that remained even after Prohibition ended.

In the years after the Second World War, the American soda fountain was changing more rapidly than it had in the

Woman seated at a soda fountain table, pouring alcohol into a cup from a cane during Prohibition, 1922.

'It's Gingervating!' In this 1939 advertisement, Canada Dry Ginger Ale 'picks you up' (sugar) and 'aids digestion' (ginger).

past. There's a 1953 Norman Rockwell painting that shows a very young soda jerk (the young operator of a soda fountain) basking in the admiration of three little girls and a puppy, none of it grand or shiny at all, and even that image was part of the American nostalgia that was Rockwell's métier. By 1953 it was increasingly likely that a soda fountain would be a Formica

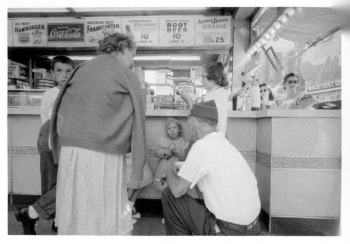

People gathered at simple soda fountain/lunch counter, New York, 1958.

counter in a luncheonette or lunch diner or a Woolworth's store. The soda fountain became part of the new teenage culture developing at the time. High school kids could meet or go on dates there. There were still people who delighted in soda-fountain lingo – 'hail' meant ice cubes, a 'black and white' was (in some places) a chocolate soda with vanilla ice cream, and a 'Cold English' was a glass of iced tea. But many towns were changing. For the United States, the post-war period brought a new world of suburbs and automobiles, of home refrigerators and bigger supermarkets, and fast-food establishments. The existing 'old time' soda fountains, from whatever era, were cherished (or, more likely, rejected) as places from the past.

3
Around the World
in a Soda Bottle

Although soda was dispensed from fountain equipment in countries other than the U.S. – or fizzy drinks were mixed with siphons – it was only in America that shops containing soda fountains became central institutions of the nation's culture. When American trade journals discussed exporting fountain equipment or syrups to other countries, they admitted that they were not having much success. In South America, they said, people weren't interested in the soda fountain because they wanted to sit and drink slowly, and talk, and the culture of American soda-fountains did not seem leisurely enough. In an article hopefully entitled 'Fountains Gain Ground in England' (1921), the writer noted, 'Britain is a country that is not over-burdened with soda fountains.' While shops that sold pastries, sweets or fruit were also selling 'drinks of the fizzy sort', he says, customers bought drinks in bottles.[1] American reference books about making carbonated drinks most often addressed the needs of the soda fountain; similar books in England were largely concerned with mixtures that could be bottled. In the very back of an English book for bottlers were 'American syrup recipes', which used real fruit. They could not be bottled.

There were some countries other than the United States to have soda fountains. Canada had soda fountains like the

Shop front and interior of the New York Marble Bar and Ice Cream Parlor, Queen Street, Brisbane, *c.* 1912. Aspirational and over-decorated soda fountains were 'American' – even when, like this one, they were in Australia.

American ones and manufactured soda-fountain equipment. In Australia, there was a 1912 soda fountain that, inside and out, looked exactly like the American examples: it was called the 'New York Ice Cream Shop'. Similarly, Barcelona had, one hundred years later, an establishment called 'American Soda'. They were, outside the United States and Canada, novelties. Other places had cafés, bars, tea shops and piazzas as meeting places, and the American-style soda fountain, with its excesses of decor and drinks, never fully caught on. As the French newspapers said after the Exposition Universelle, it was all very American. But sweet fizzy drinks were certainly available across the Western world.

By 1900 fizzy drinks were available on every continent except Antarctica. That doesn't mean everyone drank them – they didn't – but they were there, brought by, shipped to or bottled for colonists, immigrants, tourists, soldiers and locals. It bespeaks a period of early globalization, although we don't often use the term to describe the movement of people, goods and technology at the turn of that century – and in a period that pre-dates the international distribution of the famous colas. World Fairs, steamships and trains moved equipment and ideas around the world more quickly than ever before.

American, British and Irish people abroad missed their lemonade and ginger drinks, and so these flavours showed up around the world, just as Italian immigrants brought their taste for fizzy *chinotto* (very, *very* bitter orange) to Canada, Australia, the United States and Germany, and then started producing dark coffee soda in Brooklyn. The turn of the twentieth century was a period of mass migration, so of course people brought their flavour preferences with them.

Many of the flavours available in the late nineteenth century and the beginning of the twentieth century were still

Manhattan's Hester Street on the Lower East Side was a neighbourhood of Jewish immigrants. In this photograph by Maurice-Louis Branger, 1914, a storefront advertises 'Cold Soda Water and Candy' (top left). Apart from ice cream (seen in the centre), street vendors also sold food and drinks.

the ones of Mayhew's London and America's earliest, simplest soda fountains: root beers and sarsaparilla, lemonade (a fizzy drink, except in the United States), a variety of fruit-flavoured sodas and 'kolas' or 'champagne kolas' that pre-dated the colas familiar to modern drinkers, and which did not at all resemble them. The older, 'golden', ginger ale, created in Ireland by Joseph Cantrell in the 1850s, travelled to North America and, in 1907, Canadian John McLaughlin developed a lighter ale called Canada Dry. The 1905 German company Sinalco ('without alcohol') exported its lemony fizz all over Europe, and then all over the world. There were also soda flavours related to the local tastes or traditional drinks of a region. By 1887 there was a green, tarragon-flavoured Georgian soda that is still popular in Russia and the Balkans. There was 'coco pine' (coconut pineapple) flavour in Cape Town, South Africa (bottled for the soldiers of the Boer War), sorrel in Jamaica and passion fruit in South Australia.

It was, by 1900, relatively easy to mix carbonated water and flavoured syrup. Still, fizzy drinks are a silly thing to ship around the world if there is an alternative. They are heavy, and virtually all that weight is water. Genuine mineral waters have to come from the source; anything else can be bottled near where it's going to be consumed. Schweppes shipped bottles of sparkling waters, tonic water, ginger beer and sparkling lemonade as far away as the East and West Indies and the Cape of Good Hope; but by 1877 it had a bottling plant in Sydney, and by 1885, in Melbourne, Australia, and Brooklyn, New York.[2]

Sinalco advertisement seen on the side of a building in this photograph of Berlin's Spittelmarkt by Waldemar Titzenthaler, 1909.

Advertisements for Sinalco.

Bottling could be accomplished on a small scale by immigrants or local entrepreneurs. There were old European companies (among them, Lorina, a lemonade, 1895; Portuguese orange Laranjada, 1872; and Joseph Cantrell's ginger ale in the 1850s), but it's clear that both bottling technology and the drinking of fizzy drinks were international. Hamoud Boualem in Algeria began bottling cloudy lemonade in 1898 (and still does). A company called Postobón has made a Kola Champagne in Colombia since 1904. (It was neither a cola nor a champagne; both terms appear in Central and South American fizzy-drink names, and nineteenth-century formularies use the term 'champagne' for drinks that have no alcohol.) Pedro Baptista de Andrade began making guarana soda in

Lagidze Waters, the famous Georgian 'lemonade' (the generic term for fizzy drink in several languages), was created by Mitrofane Lagidze in 1887. The syrups shown here are lemon, tarragon, chocolate and pomegranate.

Brazil in 1921. (Guarana, from which local peoples had made a kind of tea, is a caffeine-rich fruit.) Swedish *julmust* (Christmas juice) and *påskmust* (Easter juice) have been brewed since 1910 by the Roberts family, who wanted a good-tasting non-alcoholic replacement for beer.

The distribution of fizzy drinks could expand only when companies found ways to avoid the problems that had dogged earlier mineral-water bottlers. Bottles exploded and bottles leaked. They ruined the product and, sometimes, maimed or killed people. Early ginger-beer bottles, like early beer bottles – anything brewed or carbonated is especially volatile – were

Automatic power crown machine invented by William Painter in the late 1890s, with a capacity of 90–100 bottles per minute. It was known in the bottling trade as the 'Jumbo'.

Patent drawing for the Hutchinson's spring stopper, 1879.

often made of stoneware. Their corks had to be wired on by hand. Early glass bottles were blown – into moulds, but by hand – in a slow, labour-intensive process. The Hamilton bottles Schweppes used had rounded bottoms and lay on their sides so that their corks didn't dry out, but, still, bottles of aerated drinks sometimes exploded when shipped, or broke while they were being washed or filled. The original refundable bottles were an attempt by the bottlers to get their bottles back. (The heavy bottles cost more than their contents did.)

Throughout the nineteenth century, more than 1,000 patents were registered in the United States alone in an effort to create closures for soda bottles, a task made even more difficult by the fact that the handmade bottles were not all exactly the same size or shape. Corks – inserted with tongs, hit with a mallet, wired on and covered with foil – still leaked eventually. One method of sealing bottles that gained some popularity was invented by Hiram Codd of London in 1870, and involved blowing thick bottles with a chamber in their neck. The bottle was then sealed with a marble made of rubber, metal or glass *inside* the chamber, the carbonation of the drink holding the marble in place; opening a Codd-neck bottle required forcing the marble into that chamber in the neck. As a slightly overcomplicated way of constructing a bottle and stopper, it was surprisingly long-lived; in fact, some companies still use them.

The Hutchinson bottle of 1879 utilized a rubber disc on a wire stem as a stopper. It had the advantage of being resealable, since the shape of the bottle prevented the disc from falling to the bottom. Only in 1892 was the Hutchinson stopper replaced by a new invention: the 'crown cork', invented by William Painter of Baltimore, Maryland, which is the one that most of us know as a bottle top. A process for fully automated manufacture of bottles was not patented until 1898.

Keeping the ingredients of the bottled drinks stable also presented challenges that soda fountains didn't face. At the time of the Hutchinson bottle, for instance, bottlers could make their own extracts, by soaking fruit in alcohol, and were likely to limit their offerings to 'red, white, black, and brown lines' – strawberry, lemon, sarsaparilla and cream soda – plus ginger ale and maybe a speciality or two. They could also order natural extracts, or, as at soda fountains, they could order artificial flavours. In the American *Treatise on Beverages; or, The Complete Practical Bottler* (1888), Charles Herman Sulz waffles mightily on the subject of artificial flavours, torn between their inferiority and their convenience and stability.[3]

There are few instances in which we can see how fizzy drinks were received in places where they had been unknown. Japan, a country that had no tradition even of iced drinks, encountered soda shortly after being forcibly opened to the West in the 1860s. Fizzy lemonade was introduced so early that some Japanese people still credit Commodore Matthew Perry with having brought it. Although Perry may have been carrying lemonade as an antiscorbutic for his crew, it was first offered for sale in 1872 by the Scotsman Alexander Cameron Sim at his pharmacy in Kobe, where it was served to the expatriate community and then, after advertising it in the local paper as a preventative against cholera, to the Japanese.

Even today Japanese people have mixed feelings about carbonation, yet they embrace fizzy lemonade. In Japanese, 'lemonade' sounds roughly like 'Ramune' ('RAH moo nay') – and sodas called Ramune made by multiple companies remain popular in Japan. Ramune was attractive, in part, because of its bottles – the Codd bottles with the marble closure – which have the added novelties of making it hard to open, hard to drink (one must negotiate around the marble) and so funny-looking that some children called it 'alien head' soda. Also, the marble rattles while you drink and sounds like a wind chime. Travellers reported little old ladies pulling Ramune out of a cold well for them in 1918; and some Japanese remember, with

Grocery store shelf with bottles of Ramune sodas in their Codd bottles, Alameda, California.

Nakamura Tsune, *Still-life with Calpis Wrapping Paper*, 1923, oil on canvas.

nostalgia, drinking 'marble soda' before the Second World War. It comes in about 45 flavours now and is also available in larger plastic – PET (polyethylene terephthalate) – bottles, but much of its appeal lies in the archaic Codd bottle.

Ramune was not an anomaly for Japan, as it turned out. In 1884 the Japanese began producing Mitsuya Cider (in Japan, 'cider' refers to any clear, carbonated soft drink; it isn't the apple juice of the u.s., nor the alcoholic product known in Britain) and it was originally sold in beautifully decorated metal bottles. Packaging is important in Japan and considerable creativity is brought to the packaging and selling of even inexpensive products. In 1919 the lactic-acid-based drink *Calpis* (called Calpico in English, to avoid the unfortunate associations of 'pis') went on the market after the founder of the company, who was on a business trip to Mongolia, encountered the cultured-milk product most often called 'kumis'. Calpis can be mixed with hot or cold water, or with sparkling water. The original design of its package – white dots on a blue background (now blue on white) – represented stars, because Calpis was introduced as a drink for a summer festival during which people look at the stars. The Japanese embraced the foreign fizzy drinks, but made them their own.

All over the world, there are soft-drinks companies that began in the late 1880s through to the 1920s. Some became national drinks, such Inca Kola, from Peru, created by the British immigrant José Robinson Lindley, who had opened a bottling plant in 1910. (Although flavoured with lemon verbena, Inca Cola tastes of bubble gum to the uninitiated.) Guaraná Antarctica has been made in Brazil since the 1920s. In Australia in 1876, the English immigrant William Bickford opened a pharmacy; after his death, his wife and son expanded their family company to include 'aerated waters'. Besides their cordials and bitters, they sold ginger ale; lemonade; 'the great blood purifier, sarsaparilla'; a summer tonic 'recommended by the medical profession' but otherwise not described in their advertisements; and 'eau de Seltz', which is what seltzer water evidently becomes when you hire a Frenchman to oversee your aerated drinks production. The Bashew brothers bottled soda for English soldiers during the Boer War in Cape Town. India, too, still sells fizzy lemonade and rose sodas in Codd bottles: 'marble soda', which is *goli* (in the south) or *banta* (in the north).

Among the famous English brands, Robert Barr created Iron Brew – now, of course, Irn-Bru – in 1901 as one of the growing number of tonics with secret ingredients. Vimto was another. Vimto was created and bottled by John Joel Nichols (a wholesale pharmacist and herb importer) in 1908 in Manchester. Originally called Vim Tonic, it is one of the many beverages that were both temperance drinks and health tonics – as in the phrase 'vim and vigour' – and it is flavoured with grapes, raspberries, blackcurrants and herbs and spices, for a total of 29 ingredients, some of them secret. It's another

Inca Kola, created in 1935 by a British immigrant to Peru who had founded a bottling factory there in 1910.

The facade of the Polo Norte soda factory, Puerto Rico. The company was founded in 1902.

drink that can be consumed hot or cold, fizzy or flat. Although native to Britain, it is also very popular in Saudi Arabia and other Middle Eastern countries, and among Muslims in general. It provides one example of how the soft drink of one region becomes established in another. In 1924 a representative of a shoe-polish company (who was a friend of Nichols's)

The Vimto factory on Ayres Road, Old Trafford, Manchester, 1928.

carried samples of the drink to the British colony of India to see if any bottling plants were interested in it. Produced at first for sale to the British troops – that ordinary pattern of homesick people longing for familiar flavours when abroad – it then became popular with the Indian peoples. Then, in 1928, at a time when Indians were travelling to the Gulf region as clerical workers, an Indian employee of a large Saudi business brought the drink to his employers, who bought the recipe from the Nichols family and began producing it, eventually adapting it to local tastes by adding date paste and making it sweeter. Vimto is now an immutable part of *iftar*, the meal that breaks the fast each night during Ramadan; and every year there are elaborate displays of it in stores in nearly forty predominately Muslim countries. Editorials praise 'that sweet berry taste of your childhood iftar memories'. It is familiar and reassuring, full of sugar and meaning. McDonald's Arabia also makes a Vimto McFizz, and one can buy bottles of Vimto encrusted with Swarovski crystals. This coming together of chance, salesmanship, fit and elaboration appropriately leads to the subject of the colas, and Big Soda.

Hires Root Beer trade card.

4
Big Soda

After the American Civil War, proprietary sodas began to be big business in America, and then big business across the globe – a state of affairs inextricably tied to cola, and particularly to Coca-Cola. Coke is a kind of measuring tool against which other drinks are compared: the Scots are pleased to tell us that they drink more Irn-Bru than Coke; Peruvians say the same about Inca Kola. Beginning in 1968, 7-Up (a lemon-lime soda in 1929) began to advertise itself as the 'uncola'. Yet cola came to dominate the fizzy industry relatively late in its history. It was not until about 1920 that colas outsold lemon drinks in Britain and ginger ale in the United States. But when colas did begin to dominate, they changed the world of sodas. They came to epitomize proprietary fizzy drinks, a category that was still new when Coca-Cola first took the stage.

Hires Root Beer illustrates an early path that soda took, en route from a homemade beverage to something that one could buy in a bottle or at a soda fountain. In 1876 a Philadelphia pharmacist named Charles E. Hires created a blend of roots and berries that families could brew into a reliable root beer. The home-brewers still had to add water, sugar and yeast – but at least they could buy all the ingredients in one packet rather than sourcing them separately. Having been persuaded not to call it a 'herb tea' (he was advised that men wouldn't buy something called a tea), he billed it as 'the Nation's Temperance Drink', and he handed glasses of it out at the Centennial Exposition in Philadelphia. That was the same exposition in which Tufts and Lippincott were selling fizzy drinks from their 10-metre-high (33 ft) fountain, but, notably, they weren't selling branded drinks: there weren't any to sell.

By 1884 Hires offered a liquid extract that could be brewed or mixed with soda water at home or in soda fountains, and by 1892 a bottled version of the carbonated beverage was in production. He also sold 'Hires Automatic Munimaker' to soda fountains. It dispensed his root-beer syrup and carbonated water at the same time, from a branded countertop dispenser into a branded mug.

Hires brought together the tradition of home brewing, herbal medicines and temperance drinks, but added an unprecedented amount of advertising: for ten years he spent

Dr Pepper advertisement, *c.* 1949. The numbers on the bottle cap refer to the company's slogan at that time: 'Drink a bite to eat at 10, 2, and 4.' The drink is supposed to provide energy in-between meals.

most of his profits on trade cards (which were still new and exciting), newspaper adverts, signs and posters. It was America's first branded root beer and one of its first branded national fizzy drinks. Many others became famous later, such as pharmacist Charles Alderton's 1885 creation of a carbonated drink that would be called Dr Pepper. It boasted of 23 ingredients in its secret recipe. Neither a fruit drink nor a cola in flavour, Dr Pepper was advertised as 'solar energy-liquid sunshine' that would provide 'vim, vigor, vitality' *and* it was a brain tonic.

Coca-Cola was just one of the late nineteenth-century American sodas to have a secret recipe, big claims and a giant advertising budget. But in 1886 there was nothing to predict that it would become *the* global soda. In retrospect, we can identify reasons why that shouldn't have happened: unlike fruit-flavoured sodas, it should be drunk very cold. Its taste was so unlike the more familiar fruit- or herb-flavoured drinks that many people initially didn't like it. When the Coca-Cola Company wants to penetrate a new market, they find it advisable to introduce fruit flavours rather than cola. Coca-Cola overcame all of these disadvantages.

While it is impossible to write about fizzy drinks without writing about colas, it is also not possible in a book of this size even to begin to address all that has been said and written on the subject. And yet, if we look at how flavoured fizzy waters acquire meanings and become big business, how they become something that people think about and have deep feelings about, we can scarcely omit Coca-Cola. Fans sometimes collect memorabilia and advertisements relating to all their favourite drinks, but there are people who decorate their entire kitchen in Coca-Cola-themed objects – including the appliances. The company has, as we will see, been consciously in

This Coca-Cola serving tray, 1950, says 'sign of good taste.'

the business of meaning-making almost since it was founded. It's succeeded.

The beginning of Coca-Cola was fairly banal. John S. Pemberton of Atlanta, Georgia, had been making patent medicines for years, and he was one of the many imitators of a product called 'Vin Mariani', a French cocaine-spiked wine. The Peruvians had traditionally chewed coca leaves; when the active ingredient, cocaine, was isolated by doctors in the mid-1800s, they used it as an anaesthetic. Angelo Mariani, the pharmacist to one of those doctors, began to experiment with combinations of cocaine and ingestible substances. (Some of these became indigestible substances: Mariani invented cocaine pâté, which sounds terrible.) Vin Mariani, cocaine in fortified wine, was a huge success. French writer Émile Zola called it 'the Elixir of Life, which combats human debility, the real cause of every ill – a veritable scientific fountain of

Coca-Cola vending machine, Kansas City, Missouri, 1952.

youth, which in giving vigour, health and energy would create an entirely new and superior race.'[1] It is a collection of claims guaranteed to warm the heart of any patent-medicine maker.

In 1885 Atlanta voted to 'go dry'. No wine allowed. Pemberton added caffeine derived from the West African *Kola acuminate* tree, but kola was intensely bitter. The result was

Man selling kola nuts at a market, Senegal.

saleable as a medicine at 75 cents to $1 a bottle, but Pemberton wanted something that could be mixed with fizzy water and sold for 5 cents a glass at Atlanta's soda fountains. That required getting rid of all but a trace of the bitter kola and substituting synthetic caffeine purchased from a pharmaceutical house. He made a sugar and water syrup, and then went about flavouring it. The secret isn't entirely what he put into it – Coke's 'secret recipe' was always in part a marketing ploy – but how he decided what to put into it. Frederick Allen describes the process of formulating the syrup, but not how Pemberton arrived at the flavour that would come to be called cola – a flavour that has nothing to do with that of cocaine or kola. Allen describes Pemberton adding lime juice, citric acid and phosphoric acid, ingredients that soda fountains used to make a drink tangy and to balance sweetness.[2] Caramel colour hides impurities. The rest of the ingredients included vanilla extract, elixir of orange, oils from lemons, and a variety of spices including nutmeg, coriander, neroli (distilled from orange flowers) and 'Chinese cinnamon' (oil of cassia), but I'd love to know what Pemberton tried and rejected. What we recognize as 'cola flavour' is a combination of these ingredients: all items that pharmacists had readily available at the time. (The flavour that would become Dr Pepper – which originated in Waco, Texas, in 1882 – bears a kind of family resemblance to cola but is fruitier.)

Pemberton took partners, including Frank Robinson, who named the drink, promoted it and wrote out 'Coca-Cola' in the script we recognize today, even as Pemberton continued to modify the recipe. As Pemberton's health deteriorated, he gradually sold his shares of the business. Asa Candler, a pharmacist and patent-medicine manufacturer, had learned about it from Robinson, and eventually came to own it. Much of what Coca-Cola became was due to Candler.

Advertisement for Coca Cola, *c.* 1900. An elegant girl sips Coca-Cola at a soda fountain.

Candler believed that Coca-Cola should be sold *everywhere* – although by everywhere, he meant at all soda fountains, even though soda-fountain owners initially resented the new 'patent drinks' such as Coca-Cola and Moxie. One of Candler's sons said that his father had 'an almost mystical faith' in Coca-Cola.

A fundamentalist Methodist, Candler brought religious zeal to the making and marketing of his product, hinting, in a 1900 letter to his son, of future world domination. (The vision did not, famously, include putting the drink in bottles, which, at the turn of the century, led to a system of franchised Coca-Cola bottlers that was modified only in the mid-1980s.[3] His

A celebrity endorsement for Royal Crown Cola by the famous actor Irene Dunne, 1942. Royal Crown Cola didn't have the cachet of Coca-Cola or Pepsi, but Ms Dunne said it tastes best.

reluctance to bottle it was based on the part of American soda history that the Coca-Cola company will later disavow: for all the emphasis through the years on soda, especially Coca-Cola, as 'democratic', Candler believed that bottling it would make Coke less genteel.)

Other companies immediately began to formulate colas, based on that same basic combination of citrus, spice and vanilla. In 1898 'Brad's Drink', a cola created by Caleb Bradham of North Carolina, was renamed 'Pepsi-Cola'. What is now 'RC Cola' began as Royal Crown, a company in Georgia. By the turn of the twentieth century, there were about eighty named colas in the U.S. and formularies – recipe books for people running soda fountains – had many more.

Candler was not averse to taking advantage of some of cola's more extravagant associations, which were based on the ingredients for which it was named, nor did he advertise when he and Robinson removed much of the cocaine in 1891. He didn't want to give up the claim that it had that potent and exciting substance in it, but, at the same time, what had been a common ingredient and a wonder drug was increasingly falling into disrepute. At the same time, in order to legally call it 'Coca-Cola', the drink was required to contain at least token amounts of those substances: a tiny bit of coca leaf with the active ingredient removed. During a trial in 1901, Candler himself stumbled over the question of whether the drink contains cocaine, hence the historical uncertainty about the presence of cocaine in Coca-Cola.[4] Candler stopped marketing it as a tonic in 1898, because at that time tonics became subject to a new tax. Nearly 10,540 hl (281,000 gallons) of Coca-Cola syrup were sold in 1899.

Candler's gift was that he was the first of many soda-makers to understand how important branding and advertising were going to be. He made sure to hang on to the patented name, suing obvious imitators like Coco-Cola and Kola-Coca. The name had to remain linked to his product. And he advertised on a scale that had never been seen, for any product. In *For God, Country, and Coca-Cola*, the definitive history of the drink and the company, Mark Pendergrast says that in 1913 the company distributed over 100 million pieces of advertising including 'thermometers, cardboard cutouts, and metal signs (50,000 each), Japanese fans and calendars (a million each), 2 million soda fountain trays, 10 million matchbooks, 20 million blotters, 25 million baseball cards and innumerable signs made of cardboard and metal'.[5] By 1914, there were, in addition, approximately 46,500 m² (5 million sq. ft) of signs painted on the fronts and sides of buildings, sometimes covering the whole side of a building.[6]

Bill Backer, who created some of Coca-Cola's best-known campaigns, including the iconic 1971 television advert, said, 'The product of the Coca-Cola Company is not Coca-Cola – that makes itself. The product of the Coca-Cola Company is advertising.' Or, as one advertiser put it, 'We're selling smoke. They're drinking the image, not the product.'[7] A major Pepsi-Cola executive said the same thing. This is, finally, one of the great truths about how fizzy drinks gain a following and establish an image. For Coca-Cola, the statement underlay some of the policies that would make it a giant. The company made its 'secret' formula syrup, but not — once it started to be bottled by franchisers in 1899 – the drink. Although the company supply its syrup to bottlers, the bottlers themselves supplied the sugar, the water, the bottles and the bottling plants.

In 1920 Coca-Cola settled a series of cases based on the premise that if the drink contained neither cola nor cocaine, it was, under the United States's new 1906 Pure Food and Drugs Act, falsely labelled, notwithstanding Candler's efforts to avoid this problem by including token amounts of these substances. But the outcome of the case demonstrates the success of the company's marketing. The U.S. Supreme Court Justice Oliver Wendell Holmes Jr held that the name

> now characterizes a beverage to be had at almost any soda fountain. It means a single thing coming from a single source, and well known to the community. It hardly would be too much to say that the drink characterizes the name as much as the name the drink . . . it has acquired a secondary meaning.[8]

That was quite an endorsement.

The United States was full of big red Coca-Cola signs and, by 1913, 190-ml (6½-oz) 'hobble-skirt'-shaped bottles that were as easy to distinguish as the company's logo. By 1926 there were almost one hundred bottlers in 78 countries, and Robert Woodruff (the company's president from 1923 to 1954, although he maintained considerable control until his death in 1985) had created a new foreign department. The company's ability to expand abroad – *before* the major expansions of the Second World War or, later, of fast-food restaurants – began to demonstrate how 'Big Soda' would operate. For example, in 1939, as part of a trade agreement, the Brazilian government agreed to change its laws so that Coca-Cola could include phosphoric acid (heretofore forbidden) and to reduce the taxes on 190-ml bottles at a time when Brazilian soda manufacturers used bigger bottles. Brazil's own guarana soda did not need the phosphoric acid or colouring agents that Coca-Cola would be permitted to operate with and the local soda companies would henceforth, in effect, be penalized for selling their drink in the bottles they had always used. Even though Coca-Cola was virtually unknown in Brazil, the Coca-Cola company was able to benefit at the expense of the local manufacturers, profiting from laws it had helped to create. Coca-Cola wanted to dominate the fizzy-drinks market. It was during the Second World War that Coca-Cola came to be equated with America and American values – and capitalism.[9]

Because of sugar rationing and other restrictions, the British soft-drinks industry was condensed into the Soft Drink Industry (War Time) Association. Only cordials could be produced, and all soft drinks were sold under generic wartime Soft Drink Industry (SDI) labels, with the companies dividing the profits. Vimto thus became a SFC of the SDI: a speciality-flavour cordial of the soft-drinks industry. Although the Minister of Food, Lord Woolton, wanted soft drinks to be available during the war, he wanted them produced in as streamlined a manner as possible.[10]

At a time when American soda companies also experienced sugar rationing, Coca-Cola expanded. Robert Woodruff promised, 'every man in uniform gets a bottle of Coca-Cola for five cents, wherever he is and whatever it costs our company', and he proceeded to make that possible.[11]

Woodruff had support in high places. President Franklin D. Roosevelt said that soft drinks were 'part of our way of life'; American generals Eisenhower, MacArthur and Patton argued that a Coca-Cola shortage would 'cause an increase in the consumption of alcohol'. Coca-Cola, they said, was necessary to sustain morale among the troops. Its years of ubiquity in America had established it as something desirable to homesick GIS. Historically, Coke campaigns were (and are) based on getting people to create their own associations to the product and to feel that they are making it 'theirs'. When the military encouraged soldiers to ask for products by brand – cigarettes as well as soft drinks – the soldiers asked for Coca-Cola.

Coca-Cola was permitted to designate 148 bottling plant technicians as 'Technical Observers' in military uniforms. The u.s. government paid most of the expenses for the building of 64 bottling plants across Europe, North Africa, Australia and the Far East – wherever American soldiers went. (One plant was dismantled and flown across the Himalayas.) Having been given the same priority as food and munitions, Coca-Cola for GIS was exempt from sugar rationing.

Thus, for some of the millions of military personnel, Coca-Cola was equated with home, with America and – for some – with freedom. One soldier said, 'If anyone asked us what we are fighting for, we think half of us would answer, "the right to buy Coca-Cola again – as much as we want".' The Coca-Cola company claimed that the war had made customers of 11 million soldiers and expanded the overseas market in a way that otherwise might have taken 25 years.[12] It brought Coca-Cola to people who had never tasted it – or any other

A 'technical observer' in a quasi-military uniform supervises the Coca-Cola packing department in India during the Second World War, 1942.

soda – before: Zulus, Fiji Islanders, native people in Papua New Guinea. The company said, 'Anything the American fighting man wanted and enjoyed was something [others] wanted,' and resulted in 'the almost universal acceptance of the goodness of Coca-Cola'.[13]

The 'goodness' of Coca-Cola may, however, not have had much to do with its flavour. Some people had drunk Coca-Cola before and hadn't liked it, but they appreciated the sweet, cold drink delivered by the American GIs who were liberating their homes, in parts of the world that had sugar rationing, danger and no way to keep anything cold. Also, one of the technical observers noted that 'anything with sugar in it was currency on the black market.'[14]

Coca-Cola's worldwide rise was based on availability, associations, caffeine and sugar. Because of its advertising before the war, it was familiar to the soldiers. Because Coca-Cola and the U.S. government arranged for Coca-Cola to be available to soldiers during the war, its identity as 'American' was reinforced, for U.S. soldiers and for the peoples with which they came in contact. Thus, in the years after the war, Coca-Cola's reach expanded based on people's wartime experiences of it and on the wartime establishment of government-financed overseas bottling plants.

The power of its identification as American eventually gave it a place in the Civil Rights movement of the 1960s. When young Black protesters 'sat-in' at a 'whites only' lunch counter in 1960, they ordered, and were denied, Cokes and hamburgers, symbols of what it meant to be able to participate in American culture.[15]

After the Second World War, and particularly during the 1960s, there was what historian John Burnett calls a 'cold drinks revolution' in Britain, comparable to the 'hot drinks revolution' three hundred years earlier, when coffee, tea and chocolate had gained in popularity. Burnett points to the increasing numbers of people in Britain who had central, or at least improved, heating systems after the war and so, he argues, were more likely to consume a cold drink, rather than a hot drink to keep them warm.[16]

This revolution began earlier in the United States, which enjoyed post-war prosperity while Britain was struggling to rebuild and was still subject to rationing. The U.S. government-funded post-war developments that had been so hard on the soda fountain – new suburbs of single-family houses with central heating and refrigerators, and a family car in the garage – encouraged families to buy fizzy drinks at the supermarket. The period also coincided with the beginning of fast-food chains such as McDonald's.

The rise and spread of McDonald's is, like the subject of colas, bigger than the scope of this book; however, in 1955, when Ray Kroc bought the right to expand the McDonald's chain, Coca-Cola became more than the company's soft-drinks supplier. When McDonald's spread overseas, it used Coca-Cola offices until it could establish its own. Worldwide, McDonald's is Coca-Cola's biggest customer and enabled the drink to penetrate foreign markets, furthering its identification as American.

During the 1970s Coca-Cola and Pepsi became cheaper to produce and were sold in new, larger containers, leading to the rise of larger servings. First, in 1970 Pepsi became available in 2-litre (2-quart) bottles. Plastic could be made into bottles that were cheaper than glass bottles and did not have to be returned to the company. They, like the soda cans introduced in 1953, addressed Pepsi's inability to produce a bottle with the cachet of Coca-Cola's 'hobble skirt' design. And they enabled supermarket shoppers to purchase large, lightweight, resealable containers of Pepsi. Coca-Cola followed suit in 1978. In 1985, both Coca-Cola and Pepsi were available in 3-litre (3-quart) bottle. Coca-Cola experimented briefly with 4-litre (u.s. gallon) bottles, but the larger bottle sizes failed. An open container of soda goes flat, and it goes flat faster in a plastic container than one of glass or metal.

What made soft drinks cheaper to produce during the 1970s was the u.s. government's new policy of subsidizing corn (maize) production, in order to lower the price of milk, beef and bread. By 1974 glucose-fructose syrup (known in the United States as high-fructose corn syrup, HFCS) began to replace some of the cane sugar in American sodas; by 1984 it had replaced sugar entirely in most sodas. Glucose-fructose

Former governor of Alaska Sarah Palin drinks from a Super Big Gulp (44 oz) during her speech at the 2013 Conservative Political Action Conference (CPAC), saying 'Bloomberg's not around; our Big Gulp's safe'. Mayor of New York City at that time, Michael Bloomberg was trying to ban the sale of large sugary drinks as part of a campaign to fight obesity.

syrup is sweeter than sugar and, especially when corn is subsidized, far cheaper. Not only did bottles increase in size, but so did the individual servings sold at fast-food restaurants and movie theatres.

In the mid-1980s Coca-Cola's CEO, Roberto Goizueta, told bottlers,

Right now, in the United States, people drink more soft drinks than any other liquid – including ordinary tap water . . . If we take full advantage of our opportunities, someday, not too many years into our second century, we will see the same wave catch on in market after market, until, eventually, the number one beverage on earth will not be tea or coffee or wine or beer. It will be soft drinks – *our* soft drinks.[17]

5
The War(s) Against Soda

There has always, at any given time, been someone fighting against sweet fizzy drinks. People have fought them because of what has been (or may have been) put into the drinks intentionally – cocaine, caffeine, phosphoric acid, carbon dioxide, artificial colours, cane or beet sugar, corn-based sugars, or artificial sweeteners or flavours. People have fought fizzy drinks because of what has, perhaps, been inadvertently introduced into them, such as contaminants. Or because of what's not in them – in particular, nutrients. Objections may have been to multinational corporations ('Big Soda'): their power and their practices. There has also been opposition to what particular fizzy drinks *mean*. Coca-Cola executives have described their product as 'the nearest thing to capitalism in a bottle'[1] and as 'the sublimated essence of America'[2]; thus it is not surprising that Coca-Cola encounters resistance among people who – symbolically, metaphorically, literally – don't want to drink *that*. As one advertisement for Turka Cola put it, 'You are drinking America; you are not drinking a soda.'[3]

Some early opponents of soda believed that drinkers would be stimulated and made ill by it, even become addicted to it, because they feared the dangerous addictive power of cold drinks. An 1894 article in the *Chicago Herald* said that

The ubiquity of Coke: created to commemorate Coca-Cola's 100th anniversary in 1986, and then updated for its 125th anniversary in 2011, this logo can be found in the Chilean desert near the city of Arica. Constructed from 70,000 empty Coca-Cola bottles, it measures 50 m tall by 120 m wide.

there were ice-water addicts just as there were morphine addicts.[4] Ice water was blamed for 'American chronic dyspepsia and other stomach ailments'; the British were warned about 'the growth of the ice habit in England'.[5]

There were, and are, fears of addiction to what might be in soda. The Women's Christian Temperance Union (WCTU) fought Charles E. Hires – himself an ardent believer in temperance – because he called his product 'Root *Beer*'. They accused Coca-Cola of peddling cocaine. Dr Harvey Washington Wiley, who was largely responsible for the 1906 American Pure Food and Drug Act, sued Coca-Cola because their product did not have cocaine in it (false advertising) and then because caffeine in Coke was an additive as opposed to being a natural ingredient, as it is in coffee and tea. He was testing the boundaries of the new Pure Food and Drug Act, a precursor to modern labelling laws designed to tell us what's in ur food. For those who grew up drinking colas or other caffeinated soft drinks, Dr Wiley may seem to have been rather silly. Today, however, mainstream paediatric medicine agrees that caffeine has no place in a child's diet. Modern Coca-Cola contains one-third of the caffeine that it had before Dr Wiley intervened.

There have been concerns about the safety of colourings used in soda, and a number of colouring agents have been replaced or modified, including the caramel colouring that we associate with a cola.

There have been questions about the safety of carbonation in soda. When people first encounter carbonated drinks, they have sometimes disliked the feeling of carbonation in their mouths (like 'needles') or bloating in their stomachs. Carbonation also causes people to burp. When soda contained bicarbonate of soda, it was *intended* to make people burp, in order to 'settle the stomach'. But as we look at how people feel about soda, and why they might embrace or reject it, one of the main issues turns out to be how they feel about burping.[6]

Eastern European Jews – seltzer-sellers and drinkers in their old countries and in their new ones – consider a burp (in Yiddish, a *greptz*) a good and healthy thing. Among native peoples of Papua New Guinea, a burp is an offering to the gods. Maya peoples in South America have replaced a traditional fermented corn alcohol used for a sacred ceremony (that involves burping) with Coca-Cola and Pepsi-Cola. In churches in San Juan Chamula, Mexico, Pepsi has replaced communion wine because 'carbonation drives off evil spirits and cleanses the soul'. Burps are holy: 'When men burp, their hearts are open.'[7]

In other places, burping is a noise that people shouldn't make in polite company. Burping may be associated with uncouth, beer-drinking men, and thus with negative feelings about alcohol. Objections to loud bodily functions may cause people to reject soda altogether, or to choose one that causes fewer of these rude noises (a local Breton cola over Coca-Cola, for instance[8]). Furthermore, since burping can be associated with digestive problems, some say that carbonation should be avoided for health reasons.

The acids in soda – particularly the phosphoric acid used in many colas for taste, and to inhibit the growth of bacteria – have been challenged. As early as 1949, Europeans, particularly the French, objected to phosphoric acid because some studies associated it with heart disease, while Coca-Cola's representatives argued (pointedly) that Coca-Cola hadn't hurt 'the American soldiers who liberated France from the Nazis'.[9] The arguments dragged on until, in a 1953 court case, a judge ruled that the phosphoric acid could stay. More recently, phosphoric acid has been linked to the loss of calcium, affecting bone density and suggesting that fizzy drinks without phosphoric acid are a better choice; others have argued that milk or calcium supplements are necessary to balance it.

Some of the opposition to soda has been based on what is known to be in it; other objections have been based on not knowing or understanding what it contains. Fizzy drinks were popularized during a period notorious for the adulteration, cheapening and misrepresentation of ingredients: Mayhew described the dubious ingredients of the cheaper soft drinks sold in London; pharmacists, soda-fountain operators and bottlers shared among themselves the chemical formulas used to create artificial flavours for their drinks, but consumers weren't informed about what they were drinking. The makers of the proprietary drinks – Irn-Bru, Vimto, Dr Pepper, Hires Root Beer, Coca-Cola and others – boasted of their secret recipes. A secret can be attractive, with its suggestion of

Advertisement for 7-Up's 'lithiated' lemon soda, 1929. The label makes an unusually long lists of claims and alludes to its active ingredient, the mood stabilizer lithium citrate, which, presumably, is what 'Takes the "ouch" out of grouch'.

glamour or exclusivity, but it can also be worrying. In 1895 a New York City newspaper reported that a boy who worked at a soda fountain had told a female customer that soda contained 'marble dust, acid, gas, sugar-coated pills, giant powder, cologne water and kerosene, all mixed up together and then distilled'.[10] Bizarrely, the recipe is more accurate than it seems at first glance – the making of a fizzy drink does indeed involve marble dust, acid, gas, sugar and something that smells good – but we definitely don't want to *drink* the marble dust and kerosene. So, we might wonder: are manufacturers hiding their secrets because their product is so wonderful that everyone would want to copy it, or are they afraid to tell us what's in it?

The modern war against fizzy drinks is part of the opposition to the seeming power of sugar. It combines new concerns with old ones. When cane sugar was first introduced into Britain and Europe, it was considered a good thing – a medicine even – and then a spice, then a rather elegant, pricey plaything of the nobility. No one worried about sugar until it became cheaper and more readily available.

Although seemingly innocuous, sugar was identified as a dangerous food more than a hundred years ago, not because it was nutritionally empty – the relationship between calories and energy was one of the first nutritional concepts understood by early physicians, so sugar's calorie content was a good thing – but because it was understood to be seductive. The concern was that children who were allowed to eat cheap sweets would be both wasting their money and learning to give in to their urges rather than being taught self-control; thus there was understood to be a direct link between eating sweets and sexual promiscuity and alcoholism. (But apparently this applied only to poor children.[11])

The modern opponents to sweet drinks agree that sugar impairs self-control. They contend that sugar is addictive, particularly in liquid form, and that it is a substance for which there may not be an innate 'off' switch in the body.[12] We do worry about empty calories, however, and it is a concern to taken seriously. Still, when critics judge harshly those who drink too much soda, they potentially link themselves to a Victorian judgement of the poor. In the same way that the Victorian poor in London were sustained by, and condemned for, their meals of hot sugared tea and white bread, the rural poor of the United States have sometimes historically been sustained by a cola with salted peanuts stuffed in the neck – called a 'farmer's lunch' or a 'goober [peanut] cocktail' – or by a cola and a Moon Pie (a chocolate-covered marshmallow and graham cracker snack cake, circa 1919), called, in the 1950s, the 'working man's lunch'. Consisting of water for hydration, a stimulant, carbohydrates, salt and fat (even protein, if there are peanuts involved), and cheaply and conveniently packaged, cola was the fast food of another age and place. In Mexico today, a Gansito snack cake and a soda cost about a dollar and serve as a cheap lunch. Subsidized corn in the u.s. makes fast food, as well as soda, much cheaper to produce and to buy than healthier foods. But these observations address only the moral judgements made about people who consume quantities of sugary drinks and does not yet address the healthfulness of sugar consumption.

There has been, since the 1990s, increasing alarm over the growing quantities of sweet drinks consumed and the rise of obesity, type 2 diabetes, heart disease, tooth decay and vitamin deficiencies. There are rising levels of obesity in parts of the world that historically have had none: in parts of Africa, for instance, where some people seem to be going directly from starvation to obesity. Sweet drinks are readily available; clean water may not be. Similarly, there are rural areas in Mexico where the Coca-Cola Company bottles the available water and sells it to the poor – except that Coca-Cola is cheaper than water, and so people drink that.[13] The World Health Organization maintains that obesity doubled worldwide between

1980 and 2015, and that this correlates to the consumption of sugary drinks.

The replacement of sodas' cane or beet sugar with cheaper glucose-fructose syrup began in the 1970s. Particularly in the United States, government subsidies made the modified corn syrups much less expensive than sugar. We have, combined here, two sets of concerns. One is historical attitudes towards (and understanding of) sugar; the other, a disagreement about the safety of glucose-fructose syrup, believed by many to be even less healthy than cane or beet sugars. The switch to modified corn syrups brings together fears of unfamiliar ingredients, our struggle to understand what we're consuming, and resentment against soft-drinks manufacturers for using government subsidies.

The underlying question is whether sugary liquids are problematic because they can be drunk in large quantities without slaking hunger, making it easy for people to consume far too many calories. Additionally, fizzy drinks are associated with diets of highly processed 'junk' foods, all of which are marketed aggressively.

The underlying concern is that fizzy (and all sugary) drinks are intrinsically dangerous, and that a single drink (if it's a very sweet one) contains more added sugars than the daily maximum that the World Health Organization (WHO) recommends, and causes blood glucose to spike. Certainly, the 'energy' promised by many soda advertisements is supplied by that burst of sugar (as well as by caffeine, if the drink contains it) and is followed by a fall in blood glucose that encourages one to drink more, for more energy. But that description of a sudden rise in blood sugar assumes that people are consuming the drink by itself, on an empty stomach, and not with a meal that includes foods which are being metabolized at different rates.

Debates over the relative dangers of cane and beet sugars, corn syrups, honey, concentrated fruit juices and other sources of caloric sweeteners that are added to drinks or foods make a complicated subject even more confusing than it has to be. Notwithstanding claims to the contrary, sugar is sugar. Be it highly processed cane sugar or raw honey, the body processes pure sugar the same way.

Artificially sweetened fizzy drinks, now a multibillion-dollar business, have their own history of disputes about their safety. Beginning in the 1960s, successive generations of artificial sweeteners – cyclamate, saccharine, aspartame (E951, marketed as NutraSweet), sucralose (marketed as Splenda) – were associated with risks of cancer. Enormous amounts of information, scientific or otherwise, indicated that these were safe for long-term use, or that they were *un*safe, or that they were not, in themselves, carcinogenic, but that they were linked to weight gain and metabolic syndrome. While examination of some of the research about the intrinsic dangers of the sweeteners proved fears to be unfounded (for example, the rats developing tumours were ingesting the quantity of saccharine that, for a human, would be like drinking five hundred bottles of diet soda each day), consumers' general uneasiness, disagreement and disgruntlement remain, alongside an awareness that some of the research against artificial sweeteners was funded by the sugar companies.[14] Furthermore, researchers are still trying to account for why diet sodas may, without calories, still contribute to weight gain.[15]

Fizzy drinks may contain things that the manufacturer and bottler don't intend. Early bottled sodas were subject to the vagaries of bottling plants that didn't have a reliable way to clean the recycled bottles. People found straw, broken glass, feathers, ash, cockroaches, lead shot and cigarette butts in their bottled drinks in the late 1800s.[16]

beers and home-brewed drinks. A new and (to her) not very interesting beverage was taking the place of drinks that she liked or that she cared about as part of English history.[20]

Similarly, Chitrita Banerji lovingly describes Indian sherbet-sellers of tall cold drinks made of water, sugar, melon seeds, almonds, cashews, spices such as cardamom, anise and saffron, and flower essences; or fruits, sometimes poured over a ball of crushed ice, in contrast to drinks that were 'aerated like sodas and colas'. 'How', she asks the reader, 'can a bottle of soda, churned out by a vast manufacturing plant, slake the thirst and spike the imagination in quite the same way?'[21]

At a bar in Paris, a man in a beret spits a mouthful of Coca-Cola straight at the camera, April 1950, a clear commentary on 'Coca-Colonization'.

Here we see again the question of how we make meaning from the foods and drinks that we consume. The evidence shows that a bottle of soda can indeed 'spike the imagination', but Banerji could still question what it is that is imagined or invoked by the replacement of one soft drink by another.

The fear that cultures will be overwhelmed by outside influences is demonstrated – most famously – in the film *The Gods Must Be Crazy* (1980), in which an African tribe (the San people, also known as Bushmen), living with no knowledge of the outside world, is almost destroyed by the arrival of an empty Coca-Cola bottle dropped from a passing airplane. In this instance, it is the symbolism of the bottle that endangers a culture, in contrast to the 1912 film *For His Son*, in which the literal contents of a cocaine-laced soda called Dopokoke pose the threat.

But individuals and cultures have always taken in and absorbed 'outside' influences, because that is the nature of culture: it is not static. Italy did remarkably well with the tomato, for instance. Sparkling lemonade seems not to have done much harm in the places where it arrived with the British in the nineteenth century – Japan in particular has proved itself adept at absorbing and transforming outside cultural influences.

Anthropologist Sidney Mintz argues that there are two kinds of meaning: 'inside meaning' and 'outside meaning',[22] a concept that may be of use here. The Maya, for example, make deep, meaningful and often touching connections to Coca-Cola ('inside meanings'), but they do so in a context that is not of their own making ('outside meanings'). The ability of individuals and cultures to make their own meanings for consumer products is well understood by those involved in modern marketing, and it has long been Coca-Cola's primary marketing strategy. 'Becoming part of people's lives,

The Gods Must Be Crazy (1980, dir. Jamie Ulys). The South African film was criticized for ignoring apartheid and misrepresenting the Bush people but remains a classic fantasy of the symbolic dangers of Western culture.

belonging, is the name of the game,' said a former head of the company's international team. What does Coca-Cola's Atlanta, Georgia, headquarters make of this prayer? 'Take this sweet dew from the earth, / Take this honey. / It will give you strength on your path.' These are words spoken by Maya mothers as they offer a dead child a sip of Coca-Cola.[23] (There may well be an answer for this: the Coca-Cola Company employs upwards of fifty cultural anthropologists, ethnographers and other cultural experts.)

As a response to the policies of the countries the multinationals represent or their effect on national culture, many countries have fought back by creating competing soft drinks, especially colas, or by promoting their local fizzy drinks. Germany created Afri-Cola in 1931 as a rejection of the Coke. Elsewhere, the need to fight came later. For example, in the late 1900s, it was fashionable in the Middle East and North Africa to drink Coca-Cola, Pepsi, Sprite and so on as a sign of 'modernity and open-mindedness'. By 2004, however, these same drinks were 'a kind of attack on the cultural and religious traditions of Muslim culture in general and Iranian and Arab culture specifically'.[24] In contrast to this, Vimto, with its long association with iftar, retains its international popularity among Muslims.

Whether it was because of a rejection of foreign companies, of the unavailability of the companies' products, or the business motivation to profit from a popular drink, numerous 'alternative' colas have been created, including ZamZam (Iran), Parsi Cola (Middle East), 815 Cola (South Korea) and many others. In a Turka Cola ad campaign designed to turn upside down the idea of cola as an American drink, Americans in the advertisements drink Turka Cola and become Turkish, speaking the Turkish language instead of English.

Mecca Cola, the most famous of the anti-Coca-Colas and now distributed in 64 countries, was created in France in 2002 by Tunisian-born Tawfik Mathlouthi. After the United States invasion of Iraq, many countries, including France, protested against America's actions. In the ensuing food fight, French students poured Coca-Cola (as always, *the* American symbol) into the sewers of Paris, while the dining room of the u.s. House of Representatives took to calling French fries 'freedom fries'. Mathlouthi banned Coca-Cola in his own household but, to please his son, created an alternative cola with a red-and-white label that resembles a Coke label, but whose profits do not support the multinational company – a share of the profits, in fact, are donated to a charity that helps Palestinian children.

This creation of 'not Coca-Cola' colas is a common one. In China, Hangzhou Wahaha corporation markets Future Cola

Hungarian advertisement for Vita-Cola, *c.* 1960, produced in East
Germany in 1957 as an alternative to Coca-Cola, which was not
then available.

(sold in the United States as China Cola), 'The Chinese People's Own Cola'. In Germany and France, there are numerous small colas, many of them regionally based: Breizh Cola, for example, is a cola of the Breton region in France and uses local imagery on its packaging. Ubuntu Cola and Bio Cola (sold by Oxfam) in the UK are both fair trade and organic ('bio').[25]

To the extent that the anti-Coca-Colas divert the consumer's money from the U.S., the alternatives succeed. (Coca-Cola was sufficiently annoyed by Breizh Cola's success that it launched a campaign targeted at the drink's Breton consumers.) But if the rejection is of Western values, then a Coca-Cola lookalike may further empower the brand. Surely, all rebellious kids know that to annoy their parents, they can buy 'the real thing'.

In early 2016, surveying the 'exploding nightmare' of childhood obesity, the WHO called for special taxes on sugary drinks. Sweet drinks provide a high number of calories without nutritional benefits, and do not cause satiety, meaning that people do not lower their caloric intake to compensate for the calories consumed. The taxes, similar to those on cigarettes, are intended to limit consumption and, hopefully, result in a lower incidence of obesity and the health problems associated with it. Additionally, the money collected through these taxes can be earmarked for programmes supporting health.

Numerous nations have called for or enacted such measures.[26] Mexico, one of the largest consumers of sugary drinks, enacted a tax on sweet drinks in 2014. By early 2020 about forty countries have specific taxes on sugary drinks. Among them are France, Hungary, Chile, Samoa (and many other small island nations), South Africa, the United Arab Emirates, Norway, India, Peru, the UK and Ireland. There are differences in what is taxed. For instance, Mexico taxes sweetened iced tea and fruit juice, while many countries do not, and in August 2020 voted to ban the sales of sugary beverages and highly processed foods. Bermuda taxes sugary drinks but also diet sodas and candy. The taxes created by the UK Soft Drinks Industry Levy (SDIL) are unusual in that the tax rate is stepped: drinks with 5 g or more of sugar per litre are taxed at a lower rate than those with 8 g or more of sugar. This has resulted in national and international brands reducing the amount of sugar in drinks to be sold in the UK: Irn-Bru by more than 50 per cent, San Pellegrino by 40 per cent. In response to consumer complaints and stockpiling of the original version of their favourite drink, Irn-Bru began selling, in addition to its low-sugar version, a limited-edition 'Irn-Bru 1901', which contains more sugar than the Irn-Bru that had been sold before the SDIL. Nevertheless, some researchers believe that Britain's model is the one more likely to prove effective.[27]

In the United States, such taxes can be passed by states, cities or localities but not by the federal government. Berkeley, California; Philadelphia, Pennsylvania; and Seattle, Washington, are among those cities that have passed sugary drinks taxes, but the state of Washington then passed an initiative that prevents cities other than Seattle from creating similar taxes. New York City's Mayor Bloomberg proposal to control portion size, so that customers could not buy a single drink larger than 16 oz (approximately 500 ml), even though they could buy multiple drinks, failed. The attitude of the Second World War soldier who said that Americans were fighting for the right to have as much Coca-Cola as they wanted seems to still dominate contemporary American culture.

Attitudes towards these taxes vary widely, not surprisingly. Many of the arguments involve whether these measures are effective in reducing obesity. The taxes are criticized as

The beverage industry has fought continually against efforts to tax sugary drinks or limit drink sizes.

regressive (they disproportionately affect the poor). They are observed to be inconsistent: the human body does not process the sugar in fruit juice differently from the way it processes the sugar in a soft drink; thus, to tax a fizzy drink differently from a fruit juice is a value judgement about soda. The taxes, in fact, return us to most of the common arguments about fizzy drinks as either a pleasure or a problem.

In one area arguments against these taxes seem entirely disingenuous: when companies or consumers raise objections to the government's role in regulating (or otherwise involving themselves in) matters of consumption, they ignore the ways in which government policies have so often aided corporations and their products – from the United State's support of Coca-Cola during the Second World War to government subsidies on corn that create cheap glucose-fructose syrup. If the companies that produce a product benefit from government support and have (as the Coca-Cola Company has often said) essentially infinite budgets to advertise their wares, then allowing health agencies to weigh in on the matter does not seem unreasonable. As with the depletion of ground water or the creation of pollution, corporations profit but are not held accountable for the problems they create.

Concerns with what is 'in' fizzy drinks – literally and figuratively, in ingredients and in social meanings – account for some of the directions that beverage businesses are going today.

6

Plus ça Change

The history of fizzy drinks presents us with a series of recurring contradictions: the desire for something familiar – maybe something we're nostalgic for – vies with a desire for something novel or exotic. The desire for something healthy or 'good' vies with the desire to ignore our parents or the health experts and to indulge ourselves with sugary nonsense. We consume things, including fizzy drinks, to establish our relationship to an identity that includes others: 'foodies', or those who rebel against the 'food police', a favourite celebrity, posh people. At the same time, we also want to establish our individuality. And each of us exists somewhere on a kind of fuzzy continuum: at one end, people ever-vigilant about health; on the other, those who really, really do not want to hear one single thing more about what they should or shouldn't be consuming. Then we drift about on that continuum based on a number of factors, not all of them rational.

That is, in fact, a description of modern consumer behaviour in general, but choices concerning carbonated soft drinks can easily be fluid (pardon the pun) because the choice of a fizzy drink does not involve a long-term or expensive commitment to any product or identity. There are exceptions to that rule, of course, for instance, religious or health-based dietary restrictions or, perhaps, political associations. Otherwise, choosing a soft drink isn't like buying a car, and we can drink Ramune Hello Kitty today, Irn-Bru tomorrow and Bionade Zitrone Bergamotte soda the day after, without consequences (unless we drink too much of them, in which case there are likely to be health consequences).

For a time, the Coca-Cola Company's belief that they could sell one drink in one flavour, in one size, to the whole world seemed – if not exactly *possible* – at least something they could strive for: the world looked like a homogenizing market in which developing nations would produce more and more Coca-Cola drinkers, driving out small regional companies and their products. The whole world would have McDonald's, white bread and Coca-Cola.

Instead, after 1998, the sales of sweet fizzy drinks began to fall, especially in the u.s. and uk markets, as well as in other European countries. One of Coca-Cola's wishes had come true: their iconic drink was so readily available that their customers could drink it all day. Historically, fizzy drinks were a treat: consumed in small quantities, noteworthy, a little exciting, special. However, fizzy drinks purchased from a supermarket in 2-litre (2-quart) bottles, or available with limitless free refills at a fast-food restaurant, were none of those things. Additionally, consumer culture had changed in many developed nations. The Big Sodas meshed well with cheap, reliable fast-food culture: sugar, salt, fat. But if we think of fizzy drinks in relationship to fast *fashion*, we see something different: fast fashion involves the shift from clothing that was produced seasonally, four times a year, and was intended to last, to clothing that is sold cheaply, is designed to be worn only once or twice and is shopped for weekly, if not daily. The clothing has to be constantly changing and always new, and (more recently) they have to look good on social-media platforms.

So, the big-drinks industry faced blowback from people who didn't like the corporations (or health risks) and, additionally, from consumers who were easily bored. Companies selling fizzy drinks had to distinguish themselves from Big Soda, and the Big Soda companies had to figure out how to reach new, hard-to-please consumers in a market that was saturated and satiated with products and advertisements. But the big-drinks giants already knew how to sell to those markets because they had had a place to practice: Japan.

By the turn of the twenty-first century, Japan had been the testing ground for soft-drinks experiments for decades. In 1991 John Hunter, then president of Coca-Cola's Pacific Group, said that various companies introduced between six hundred and eight hundred new soft drinks in Japan each summer, in the hopes that some would be popular;[1] in 2007 there were about 1,500. In Japan, soft drinks had become like fashion, changing seasonally. PepsiCo and Coca-Cola launched *gentei* (limited edition runs) of flavours, exciting people's interest by making the flavours ephemeral, telling customers that they had to buy the drink right away or they would miss out. In 2007 Pepsi introduced pale-green 'Ice Cucumber' soda, which sold 4.8 million bottles in a couple of weeks, and then was discontinued, a strategy that succeeded also for Pepsi Blue (berry flavour), Pepsi Red (cinnamon) and Carnival (tropical fruit). Japanese customers could buy sodas in the flavours of traditional Japanese sweets, such as red bean and green tea, or other traditional Japanese flavours, such as shiso (a variety of mint), Mont Blanc (chestnut), wasabi and cherry blossom. There was also salty watermelon soda, Dorito-flavoured Mountain Dew and octopus-flavoured soda. Japanese vending machines sold canned coffees long before canned coffees arrived in the u.s. or the UK, and they also offered the first ready-to-drink cold teas. These choices blurred the boundaries between fizzy drinks and other soft drinks, but that blurring of boundaries was not new. The Japanese drink Calpis (Calpico elsewhere around the globe) has long been available as a liquid mixed with hot or cold water or as a fizzy drink, and since it contains lactic acid, it is a little fizzy, even without carbonation.

The Japanese interest in novelty extended to how drinks are packaged and dispensed and embraced both the archaic and new. Ramune, which is still sold in Codd bottles, with their marble closures, coexisted with soft-drinks vending machines that let customers pay with a mobile phone – cutting-edge technology when it was introduced in 2002 (and also slower than paying cash).

The Japanese were selling what the international soft-drinks industry now calls 'functional drinks'. 'Pocari Sweat' (launched in 1980 by a pharmaceutical company) was a sports drink designed to replace the water and electrolytes sweated out when exercising. Pocari Sweat was followed by 'Body Style Water' to aid in weight loss and 'Love Body', which included a herb reputed to enlarge a woman's breasts.

In a 2002 *New York Times* article, 'I'd Like to Buy the World a Shelf-stable Children's Lactic Drink', the bemused writer says of the American soft-drinks market, 'We want bottled water. We want health drinks. We want a brand-new thing we have never seen before, and three months later we want another one. We want endless choices, in dozens of categories . . . we are all becoming Japanese teenagers.'[2] It is hard to imagine that as recently as the beginning of the twenty-first century it was possible for a *New York Times* writer to be surprised and bewildered by bottled water, health drinks and the diversification of markets and products. The idea of Coke or Pepsi existing in different flavours or any fizzy drink being sold in limited-edition flavours was unfamiliar to him. *Beverage Daily* (2003), an online industry newsletter, wondered if a 'Japanization' of the soft drinks market that involved the spread west of 'elixirs' (soft drinks with nutritional benefits), iced teas and iced coffees threatened the dominance of u.s. colas.

The Big Soda companies have indeed diversified worldwide. Coca-Cola now offers thousands of drinks instead of one. It has created flavours to compete with traditional ones (for example, guarana in Brazil), or has bought old fizzy-drinks companies (the ones that sell the intensely gingery Stoney Tangawizi in Africa, Thums Up in India and Kia-Ora in the uk) and small companies that produced other varieties of drinks: for example, Zico coconut water and Honest Tea.

The companies producing big-name sodas that originally came in one flavour (Pepsi-Cola tasted like Pepsi-Cola) now create new ones constantly: Cherry Vanilla Dr Pepper, Orange Vanilla Coca-Cola, Pineapple and Passion Fruit Ribena. And they create limited-edition seasonal flavours such as Pepsi Mango (Spring 2019) and Winter Spiced Cranberry Sprite (2019). This seems like Japanization, and yet it's also like the old soda fountains, where people could always ask for flavoured syrup to be added to their cola.

Aside from selling different drinks with different names and experimenting with flavours, a drink like Coca-Cola appears in different markets with different sugar content or artificial sweeteners, amounts of caffeine and containers. Coca-Cola can be purchased in – among other receptacles – 2-litre (2-quart) plastic bottles, glass bottles and three sizes of can. The designs on some of its containers associate the drink with anything from summer to the Olympics to Harry Potter. Coca-Cola has been packaged at Christmas in spherical cans resembling Christmas-tree decorations.

on Instagram accounts and on YouTube. One online version of the Japanese advert for the bow-making, singing Coca-Cola bottles, presumably directed towards people interested in marketing, included English subtitles that said, 'The most recognized sugar water – 100 yen. A successful advertising campaign – 5 million yen. Appreciating the creativity – price-less.' (Copying a classic Mastercard advertisement – expensive if Mastercard sues.) So, there it is again: sugar water and advertising – in this instance, advertising that takes advantage of social media.

Participatory advertising (as it is called in the ad world) engages and involves some of the consumers who would probably fast-forward through adverts on TV. There are virtual communities of people who 'friend' a brand on Facebook or who participate in blogs about soda tastings and compete to find the best, the worst or the weirdest. There are sites upon which participants review new drinks or drinks from around the world, sometimes with videos of people tasting the drinks. Thus people collect the merchandise (new or old) of a favourite drink, but they also collect the *experience* of tasting as many sodas as possible, and of sharing that experience online. This fits the needs of the companies because their customers are doing the advertising for them, but it also suits customers who want not just a soft drink but something that is memorable, multisensory or social.

Technology is also employed for what Bill McKibben calls 'hyper-individualization': the prioritization of individual tastes and interests over personal connections.[3] Each person can have his or her own flavour of drink (Avery, in New England, provides this), with their own picture on the label (available from Jones), their name on the label (Coca-Cola) or a unique label (Coca-Cola again). For Ramadan, Bloomingdales in Dubai and Kuwait customizes Vimto bottles with crystals, although this is for the purpose of making it into something that can be given as a gift; it's a manipulation of packaging for a different reason.[4]

Both Coca-Cola and PepsiCo have developed soda machines that allow users to customize their drinks by choosing a fizzy drink as a base and then adding other drinks or syrups. In 2009 Coca-Cola's new 'Freestyle' computerized soda-vending machine allowed customers to create custom drinks from more than one hundred flavours of soda and syrups. The machine sent the information to Coca-Cola headquarters to aid in market research. PepsiCo's 'Spire' (2014) allowed customers to make more than 1,000 drinks. The machines are sleek and computerized, yet they harken back, oddly, to James W. Tufts's giant soda fountain at the Centennial Exhibition in Philadelphia in 1876, which also boasted of its beauty and of the large number of drinks it could dispense.

A Jones Soda RV in the desert. The company is known for its custom-labelled soda bottles as well as for its imaginative (and frequently bizarre) flavours.

Novelty fizzy drink flavours, including bacon and ranch dressing.

and Curious Elixirs (U.S.), which includes ingredients such as ginger, chilli, flowers and cucumber, but also herbs that have historically been used in Ayurvedic medicine (to boost memory, lower blood sugar or increase sex drive).

There are non-drinkers who do not want their drinks to be reminiscent of alcoholic drinks. The Church of Jesus Christ of Latter-day Saints prohibits its members, Mormons, from drinking alcohol and all hot caffeinated drinks, but allows sugar – and, as of 2012, allows cold caffeinated drinks. The Church is headquartered in Salt Lake City, Utah, and church members there are producing a new fizzy-drinks culture. Unlike observant Muslims, whose drinks traditions largely pre-date commercial fizzy drinks (while embracing Vimto), the drinks culture of the Mormons begins with modern American mainstream tastes. Both at competing shops and at private events, customers can order so-called 'dirty sodas' that are based on ordinary, commercial fizzy drinks to which are added flavoured fruit syrups and cream or coconut cream. These can be customized, and they have amusing names (the one called 'Jacob's Coat' has many colours, like the coat of the biblical Joseph), just as the old soda-fountain drinks were named as much for amusement as to identify them. The 'dirty soda' shops in Mormon communities also provide the kind of community meeting spaces that might, elsewhere, be filled by coffee shops or bars.

Some of the modern fizzy drinks distinguish themselves by claiming health – or otherwise life-enhancing – benefits. The soft-drinks industry calls them 'functionals', and they are one of the fastest-growing segments of that industry, which is not surprising: the rejection of fizzy drinks is, in part, that they are 'empty calories'; furthermore, a focus of some modern food cultures is identifying 'superfoods' and nutrients that make food function as medicine. When the beverage industry was contemplating the 'Japanization' of soft drinks, these were the drinks they were calling 'elixirs', although the Japanese had already created a legal term for them: FOSHU, Food for Specified Health Uses.

Sports drinks (Pocari Sweat, Gatorade), energy drinks (Red Bull) and specific health-promoting drinks remind us that many fizzy drinks began as health tonics or patent medicines but were renamed when government agencies began regulating or taxing health claims. For many years, a manufacturer's claim that its soft drink would make you feel different, younger, better or more energetic – that it would transform you if you consumed it – could be suggested only through advertising: through images, narratives, songs and suggestion. The actual psychoactive properties of an ingredient – the caffeine of a cola or guarana drink – weren't advertised directly. Functionals again make those claims explicit: 'drink this', companies say, 'and it will make you healthy', or sexy, or focused.

The ingredients of these drinks are based on herbal medicine, non-Western medicine and information (new or old, accurate or not) about nutrients. Some of them are fizzy versions of the herbal teas available in any health store: for example, ginger or mint to settle one's stomach. One of the Curious Elixirs contains rhodiola, which has been used in both herbal and modern medicine to treat anxiety and depression. Green tea contains antioxidants, and so, in Japan – and now in the United States – there are green-tea soft drinks. There are vitamin waters, sports drinks with potassium and electrolytes, 'Rejuvenation Water' with amino acids (UK) and drinks infused with probiotics for the good of one's intestinal health.

They are sold for health – although watchdog groups have noted the amount of sugar in these drinks, which one Australian article called 'high-priced lolly waters'. Under their fancy claims, they are, most of them, sugary drinks, and even if they contain an ingredient used medicinally, they have not been formulated as medicine.

The earliest modern fizzy drinks that were marketed as functional drinks were energy drinks. Red Bull (1987), the first famous one, was created in Austria, but it was based on an energy drink sold in Thailand. Like many of the old 'tonics', it depends on caffeine and sugar – with the addition of vitamins and a chemical compound called taurine. About 7.5 billion cans were sold in 2019, in more than 171 countries.

There are also anti-energy drinks: 'Drank Extreme Relaxation Beverage' contains melatonin and valerian root. 'Slow Cow' (from Quebec) and 'Mary Jane's Relaxing Soda' (California) both contain soothing herbal ingredients. Lava Cola, manufactured in the island nation of Vanuatu, contains kava, a sedative. In the United States, sodas containing cannabis are available, but whether the Coca-Cola Company will release one is unclear: spokespeople say the company would never sell a marijuana-infused product but would consider one that included CBD, the non-psychoactive component of marijuana.

As manufacturers of fizzy drinks attempt to make their products attractive and to distance themselves from large corporations, we find – in the drinks or in the drinkers – a collection of contradictory claims and desires.

As ever, our fascination with the novel vies with our fears about what we're consuming, although we might phrase our concerns differently now from in the past. At the turn of the twentieth century, 'hygienic' and 'sanitary' were the buzz words, and 'untouched by human hands' was a recommendation, as 'all natural' and 'organic' are now. A 'craft' soda, preferably one that has a compelling story and the makers' names and stories attached to it, may be more attractive than something from a big factory. Drinkers of craft sodas prefer that the drinks have (metaphorically) been touched by human hands, which seems to make them more personal. Additionally, small companies may be able to demonstrate that they are producing their products ethically: that they are treating their employees well and not harming the environment, for instance.

Similarly, refined sugar's whiteness was once associated with purity and an absence of contaminants. Now refined sugar seems (to many people) unnatural and overprocessed. Fashionable sugar is pale brown; honey, maple sugar and some of the plant-based sweeteners like stevia may be considered even more desirable – except when 'pure cane sugar' is contrasted with glucose-fructose corn syrup, in which case, the same (evil, fattening, mass-produced substance) is adopted by trendy or retro sodas as a selling point.

Yet another way that a fizzy drink can become desirable is for it to be an old brand or associated with a particular region. These drinks may be perceived as *authentic*, a designation that can override concerns about, for instance, sugar's empty calories. This has led to the expanded distribution of old flavours. In the United States, Moxie, Vernor's Ginger Ale, Cheerwine and Green River, originally regional brands, are more widely available. Speciality soda stores, high-end food stores and online shops sell regional sodas from around the world. The English Fentimans (from 1905) distributes traditional flavours with old-fashioned-looking labels to Americans who had never heard of dandelion and burdock or cloudy lemonade.

'More authentic' versions of a Big Soda may compete with the multinational company's official version: the Coca-Cola Company fought against Americans importing Mexican Coca-Cola, in glass bottles with real sugar. 'Dublin Dr Pepper',

Vintage and regional carbonated drinks: the selection sold at a Cracker Barrel Old Country Store and Restaurant, in North Carolina. The U.S. chain specializes in regional nostalgia.

Selection of Fentimans soda on a supermarket shelf in New York City.

a version of a Big Soda but made from the original recipe with cane sugar and sold in decades-old glass bottles from one old bottling plant, had a following so intense that lawsuits (and a movie) resulted when the parent company tried to shut it down.

An appreciation for the regional or the authentic has also resulted in countries taking renewed pride in their own soft-drink traditions or in creating new ones that reflect local preferences. An advert for Brazil's best-selling Guarana Antarctica showed a picture of the guarana fruit and said, 'Now ask Coca Cola to show you the coca tree.' The Vietnamese and Cambodian *Soda sữa hột gà* is egg yoke, sweetened condensed milk and club soda in a can. A new brand in China, Hankow Er Chang, bottles fizzy drinks in traditional – that is, 1970s – flavours such as lychee, and new ones such as sour plum, lemon and sea salt, and passion fruit with lactobacillus and

Maltextrakt, a malt-flavoured soda, is a traditional drink in Iceland.

Seller of locally made Goli soda in Saligão, India.

cherry blossom. They use bottles and labels that look old-fashioned to further contrast their drinks with the international flavours and brands. Banta, the lemon-flavoured fizzy drink sold by street vendors in North India from Codd-neck bottles, calls itself 'Delhi's local drink'; it is known as 'Goli soda' in the south.

This, however, can be complicated. India's Thums Up (cola) remains more popular than the 'Big' Colas – but it is now owned by Coca-Cola. Inca Kola in Peru and Kola Román in Colombia both identify themselves as authentic, as the drinks that flow through the veins of babies in their countries; but in the United States Inca Kola advertises that people should drink it in order to 'immerse yourself in a micro vacation'.

People who are emotionally connected to a drink may or may not know who owns it. John Nese, of Galco's Soda Pop Shop in Los Angeles, which stocks more than seven hundred different carbonated drinks – many of them from small companies – says that although currently there is enormous interest in the small brands and in diversity, big corporations remain a threat. The small companies cannot get their products on the shelves of most big shops. The global companies pay for the shelf space, and the big shops auction the shelf space to the highest bidder. As the big companies buy up the small ones, they can offer a range of products that obscures the fact that the same international corporations own the Big Colas but also the old regional ones.

Internationally, objections to soda as unhealthy and to particular sodas as the product of multinational corporations have returned fizzy drinks to their roots. Just as people once made drinks at home with fizzy water from siphons and gasogenes, so, now, they make drinks from siphons and home-carbonating systems such as SodaStream. Numerous books, articles and websites explain how to brew root beers and ginger beers, kombucha and kavass, as well as how to make shrubs and switchel. At the same time, companies in places as diverse as Japan, Italy and the United States sell these drinks, repopularized because they are historic and authentic. No one but a historian could have identified a shrub or drinking vinegar in 2010; now they're on the shelves with the ginger ale, the iced tea and, as it turns out, a number of drinks that defy categorization.

There are, for example, fizzy drinks that contain alcohol. Root beer began as a fermented, very slightly alcoholic drink; in 2012 the u.s. brand 'Not Your Father's Root Beer' returned alcohol to the drink, and others followed. As I write, the craft-beer industry is in deep distress over the new 'hard seltzers': fizzy, fruit-flavoured alcoholic drinks. They are fizzy drinks, but they are not soft drinks. And yet, fizzy drinks at soda fountains sometimes contained alcohol.

The association of carbonation with junk food, a mistrust of carbon dioxide as an ingredient and a desire for novelty have led to the creation of other drinks that complicates the boundaries among categories. This blurring of boundaries isn't new: Vimto did it in the UK, as did Calpis in Japan: they could be hot or cold, flat or fizzy. Now, although the international soft-drinks industry distinguishes 'carbonates' from juices, waters, RTD ('ready-to-drink') iced teas or coffees, and so on in their statistics, fizzy drinks have influenced other beverages, in part because people who grew up drinking them are accustomed to very sweet liquids. There are innumerable soft drinks that are non-carbonated but which otherwise resemble sodas. In 1987 Snapple (previously a juice company) bottled the first ready-to-drink sweetened and flavoured iced tea in the U.S., which made it into a sugary soft drink, minus the fizz. In the terminology of the soft-drinks industry, it was a ready-to-drink tea. But now there are carbonated and flavoured sweet iced teas, one of which is called 'iced tea soda'. Something similar has happened with coffees: a Starbucks caramel cocoa cluster Frappuccino with whipped cream isn't coffee; it's a soda-fountain drink. Both PepsiCo and Coca-Cola are selling their signature beverages with the addition of coffee (or coffee and caramel). As PepsiCo's CEO Indra Nooyi said, regarding numerous choices of drinks offered by the company's 'Spire' vending machine: 'It becomes irrelevant whether it is carbonated or noncarbonated . . . Pick a beverage, pick a base and bring *excitement* to it.'[6] Modern soft drinks, like the soft drinks of long ago, like the 'hot sodas' of the soda fountains, might be fizzy or not. They may have alcohol in them and not be 'soft' at all. They may not have sugar in them.

If we combine nostalgia, a desire to have something to post on social media (or a sense of having been isolated by social media) and an interest in novelties, we rediscover a need for special places to enjoy fizzy drinks. During the Christmas season of 2019, Fentimans introduced a pink ginger drink, created a pink gingerbread house atop a London rooftop and advertised it as 'the season's most Instagrammable installation'. It was too small and too temporary to succeed, but they had the right idea. What might work is something like the American soda fountain. Descendants of the family of Dr Physick, a very early Philadelphian soda seller, have created a Victorian-era soda fountain where costumed soda jerks serve drinks made from syrup, soda water and ingredients like those in the old soda-fountain drinks. The exotically named 'Egyptienne Egg Shake' includes orange and rose syrups, and egg. (And, the moustachioed young man who served it to me whispered, 'It's not as bad as it sounds.')

Old soda fountains are newly popular, but there are also rumours of new ones – in drugstores, some of them – because both merchants and customers need there to be something on offer that you can't order online. Starbucks with their Instagrammable drinks (the Unicorn Frappuccino comes to mind) and history of free Wi-Fi and comfortable seating can function rather like a soda fountain, even for teens who do not drink coffee. One fifteen-year-old, when asked what she drank there, answered succinctly: 'sugar'. The creation of new gathering places was put on hold by the beginning of the COVID-19 pandemic in March 2020. Perhaps real, rather than virtual, visits with friends will feel even more valuable when the pandemic is under control, many people having had a superfluity of online socializing.

Fizzy drinks today and fizzy drinks in the future are expanding their offerings based on the things they have always depended on: sweetness, memory, advertising, nostalgia, novelty and

Franklin Fountain, Philadelphia: the making of a drink.

people's desire to drink something fun and, at least part of the time, believe that it is good for them. We can roll it in our mouths and contemplate the tastes, or (consciously or not) roll it around our brains to decide whether it's what we want or who we are, perhaps based on the taste, what the packaging or advertisements look like or what we know of the company's corporate practices. This, unsurprisingly, isn't straightforward either.

In his book *Belching Out the Devil: Global Adventures with Coca-Cola*, author Mark Thomas exposes the damage the Coca-Cola Company has done all over the world, yet admits that he will forever associate the smell of Coke with his beloved grandmother, with whom he drank it as a child. And he loves its taste.

For all the changes in the technology used to create and package fizzy drinks and the growth of corporations to sell and advertise them, some things do not change.

> The number of chemical teetotal drinks is legion. They are all calculated according to their concocter's reports, to make the drinker healthier and wiser; nay, even to provide him with extra brain power, as did the vaunted Zoedone [a carbonated tonic], which contained phosphates and iron. They have their little day and another nostrum takes their place. It has, hitherto, always been so, and probably will continue, only intensified, to the end of time.[7]

Recipes

Some recipes are for making and some are for pondering. These historical recipes are not ones most people can make but they are examples of what have been made in the past.

Historical

Persian Sherbet

– from *Dr Chase's Recipes* (Ann Arbor, MI, 1864)

Pulverized sugar 1 lb. [½ kg]; super-carbonate [baking soda or bicarbonate of soda] of soda 4 ozs. [115 g]; tartaric acid [cream of tartar] 3 ozs. [85 g]; put all the articles into the stove oven when moderately warm, being separate, upon paper or plates; let them remain sufficiently long to dry out all dampness absorbed from the air, then rub about 40 drops of lemon oil, (or if preferred any other flavoured oil) thoroughly with the sugar in a mortar – wedge-wood [porcelain] is the best – then add the soda and acid, and continue the rubbing until all are thoroughly mixed. Bottle and cork tight, for, if any degree of moisture is permitted to reach it, the acid and soda neutralize each other, and the virtue is thus destroyed. A middling sized table-spoon or two tea-spoons of this put into a half-pint [250 ml] glass and nearly filled with water and quickly drank, makes an agreeable summer beverage; and if three or four glasses of it are taken within a short time, say an hour or two, it has the effect of a gentle cathartic [purgative], hence for those habitually costive [constipated] it would be found nearly or quite equal to the seidlite [(*sic.*) Seidlitz] powder, and for children it would be the pleasantest of the two.

A Very Nice Lemon Syrup
– from *Dr Chase's Recipes* (Ann Arbor, MI, 1864)

Take citric acid in powder ¼ oz [7 g]; oil of lemon 4 drops; simple syrup 1 quart [1 l]. Rub the acid and oil in three or four spoons of the syrup, then add the mixture to the remainder, and dissolve with gentle heat. Citric acid is not as likely to cause inflammation of the stomach as the tartaric, hence, its better adaptation to syrups calculated for drinks, and especially in disease.

Cream Soda: Using Cow's Cream, for Fountains
– from *Dr Chase's Recipes* (Ann Arbor, MI, 1864)

Nice loaf sugar 5 lbs.; sweet rich cream 1 qt.; water 1 ½ gills; warm gradually so as not to burn; extract of vanilla ¾ oz.; extract of nutmeg ¼ oz.

Just bring to boiling heat, for if you cook it any length of times it will crystalize; use four or five spoons of this syrup instead of three, as in other syrups. If used without a fountain, tartaric acid one quarter pound is added. The tendency of this syrup is to sour rather quicker than other syrups, but it is very nice while it lasts; and if only made in small quantities and kept cool, it more than pays for the trouble of making often.

Root-beer Essence: Ottawa or Otaki Root Beer
– from Charles Herman Sulz, *A Treatise on Beverages; or, The Complete Practical Bottler* (New York, 1888)

Oil of sassafras, wintergreen, anise, of each three fluid drachms. Cut with pumice and sugar in a mortar and gradually dissolve in nine fluid ounces of alcohol of 95 per cent (190 proof), then add by degrees nine fluid ounces of water. To this essence various additions are made to suit the taste. Extract of liquorice root or of wild cherry bark, extract of ginger, capsicum, solution of citric acid, etc., are the usual admixtures, and then the essence or 'extract' as erroneously called is made to sail as Ottawa, Otaki, etc., root-beer extract.

Don't Care Syrup
– from Emil Hiss, *Standard Manual of Soda and Other Beverages*
(Chicago, IL, 1897)

120 ml (4 oz) pineapple syrup
120 ml (4 oz) strawberry syrup
5 ml (1 sp) vanilla extract
60 ml (2 oz) port wine
1 l (1 quart) simple syrup (see recipe overleaf)

Stock Champagne Syrup
– from G. H. Dubelle, *Soda Fountain Beverages*, 4th edn (1917)

3.75 l (1 gallon) Rhine wine syrup
120 ml (4 oz) French cognac
60 ml (2 oz) cherry wine

World's Fair Fruit Champagne
from G. H. Dubelle, *Soda Fountain Beverages*, 4th edn (1917)

3 l (6¾ pints) champagne syrup (see recipe above)
240 ml (½ pint) pure black cherry
240 ml (½ pint) pure raspberry juice
120 ml (¼ pint) pure red currant juice
60 g (2 oz) citric acid

15 ml (½ fl. oz) soluble essence of lemon
15 ml (½ fl. oz) soluble extract of vanilla
7 ml (¼ fl. oz) foam syrup

Use 45 ml (1½ fl. oz) of syrup per 240 ml (8 oz) of soda water.

Modern

Simple Syrup

This is needed for most homemade sodas.

400 g (2 cup) white sugar
¼ l (1 cup) water

Combine sugar and water in a medium saucepan. Bring to a boil, stirring, until sugar has dissolved entirely. Bottle when cool. WARNING: boiling sugar is dangerous and can cause severe burns.

Cucumber, Mint and Basil Soda

⅓ l (1½ cups) simple syrup (see recipe above)
½ cucumber, peeled and thinly sliced (reserve 12 slices)
24 fresh mints leaves (plus 12 sprigs for garnish)
12 basil leaves
1.5 l (6 cups) carbonated water

Bring simple syrup to a boil in a small saucepan. Remove pan from heat and add cucumber slices, mint leaves and basil. Cover and let steep for 30 minutes. Strain syrup into a jar, pressing the solids against the strainer. Partly fill a tall glass with ice cubes. Add 2 tablespoons syrup and top with carbonated water. Stir gently to combine. Garnish with cucumber slices and mint. Repeat.
Makes 12 servings

Cardamom Sparkler
– adapted from *Imbibe* magazine, https://imbibemagazine.com

20 cardamom pods, lightly crushed
100 g (½ cup) dark-brown sugar
pinch of salt
1 l (16 oz) club soda
lemon twists for garnish (optional)

Heat the cardamom pods, sugar, salt and 0.5 l (2 cups) of water in a heavy-bottomed pot over medium-high heat. Bring to a boil and then reduce heat and simmer for 20 minutes. Strain the syrup, discarding the cardamom, and chill.

When ready to make soda, add about 120 ml (4 oz) of the syrup to a 300-ml (10 oz) ice-filled glass and top with unflavoured carbonated water. Garnish with a lemon twist.

Store any remaining cardamom syrup in an airtight container in the refrigerator for up to a week.
Makes 4 servings

New Orleans Nectar Soda
– adapted from 'Recipes and Reminiscences of New Orleans', published by the Parents Club of Ursuline Academy

For the nectar syrup:
600 g (3 cups) sugar
350 ml (1 ½ cups) water
2 tbsp vanilla extract
2 tbsp almond essence
½ tsp red food colouring

Over low heat, dissolve the sugar into the water. Bring to a boil. Cool. Add vanilla extract, almond essence and red colouring. Stir well. Store in refrigerator. Pour about an inch of nectar syrup into a tall glass. Add carbonated water.

For Nectar Ice Cream Soda:
nectar syrup (see recipe above)
1 tbsp condensed milk
1 scoop of vanilla ice cream
unflavoured soda

Pour about 2 cm (1 in.) of nectar syrup into a tall glass. Add a tablespoon of condensed milk and a scoop of ice cream, and top with soda. Stir to mix.

Egyptienne Egg Shake
– courtesy of the Franklin Fountain, Philadelphia, Pennsylvania

60 ml (2 oz) orange syrup
60 ml (2 oz) rose syrup
whole egg, beaten
350 ml (12 oz) soda water
ice

Combine ingredients. Garnish with a sprinkling of blue Nile lotus petals, and a date, bifurcated to its pit with a paring knife and placed on the glass edge.

Rosemary Plum Soda

1 very ripe plum
100 g (½ cup) sugar
120 ml (½ cup) water
3–4 sprigs fresh rosemary
seltzer water
ice

Prepare the rosemary syrup: crush rosemary gently in your hands to release oils. Mix water, sugar and whole rosemary sprigs in a medium saucepan; bring just to a boil (sugar should be dissolved). Cool, allowing the rosemary to steep in the syrup. Remove rosemary sprigs.

Slice the plum. Remove the skin if you want, but it's just for aesthetics and texture. Muddle several slices of the fruit to a pulp in the bottom of two 240-ml (8 oz) glasses. Add several ice cubes.

Pour 1–2 shot glasses of the syrup over the ice (more if you'd like a sweeter or more rosemary-ish drink). Top with seltzer to the rim of the glass and give a quick stir.

In this recipe, the plum taste is mild, leaving the soda more herbal; add more plums, if you want it to be fruitier.

Indian Paneer Soda

100 g (½ cup) sugar
200 ml (¾ cup) plain water
3 drops rose essence
unflavoured sparkling water

Bring sugar and plain water to a boil. Boil on medium for 3 minutes. Cool down. Add rose essence and stir 3–4 tablespoons (to taste) over a little ice. Add sparking water and mix.

Rose water can be stored in an airtight bottle, but drink immediately after mixing.

More-or-less-Japanese Homemade Melon Soda

For the melon syrup:
1 kg (2 lb) honeydew melon, seeds and rind removed, cut into medium pieces
2 cups simple syrup (see recipe above)

Place the honeydew pieces in a food processor or a blender. Process until very smooth. Strain the honeydew puree through a medium sieve placed over a glass measure or an open airtight container. Pour in the simple syrup, and stir to combine. Honey-dew syrup may be covered and refrigerated for up to 1 day before using.

For Melon Soda:
500 ml (17 fl. oz) club soda or soda water
2 tbsp melon syrup
5–6 ice cubes
a few drops of green food colouring (optional)

Pour the soda water into a glass and add the syrup, stirring gently to mix well. You can add a few drops of food colouring. Add ice until your glass is full.

Mint Kvass
Kvass is a traditional, slightly fizzy Russian brewed drink made from stale dark-rye bread. Russian fast-food shops still sell it.

1 l (1 quart) water
100 g (3 ½ oz) black- or rye-bread slices
40 g (1 ½ oz) sugar
¼ tsp dried yeast
4 g (⅛ oz) fresh mint leaves, washed
10 g (⅓ oz) raisins or sultanas
extra mint for bottling

Dry (but don't burn) the slices of bread in an oven at 100°C (200°F) for about 45 minutes, and roughly chop. (If your oven does not operate at such a low temperature, simply leave the dough in a place in which it can dry out.) Put bread in a large bowl or jug and pour boiling water over it. Cover and cool for at least 4 hours.

Stir yeast into a little warm, sugary water in a cup. Rest for 15 minutes.

Pass the bread through a plastic sieve into a bowl, and press on bread to remove all the water. (It's the water you want, not the bread.) Crush the mint. Stir the sugar into the water from the bread. Add yeast solution and crushed mint. Cover and leave for at least 8 hours.

Place a clean cloth (tea or dish towel) in a funnel and filter the liquid through into sterilized plastic bottles. Do not use glass for fermenting. Add some raisins and fresh mint to each bottle. Cap the bottles loosely and keep them in a cool room.

After 3–5 days, filter the kvass into clean bottles. Cap the bottles tightly and store them in a refrigerator for at least 4 hours before drinking.

WARNING: THESE CAN EXPLODE.

Soda sữa hột gà (Egg Soda)
Popular in Vietnam and Cambodia.

2 tsp sweetened condensed milk
1 egg yolk
240–480 ml carbonated water (1–2 cups)
ice

Fill one glass with ice. In another glass mix the condensed milk and egg yolk. Add carbonated water to the desired level, and mix until blended well. Pour liquid over ice.

Since the egg remains raw, all the usual precautions apply.

Cola
Recipe by John Reed, pharmacist; adapted from Darcy O'Neil, *Fix the Pumps* (2010), which says, 'This is said to be an early version of Coca-Cola.'[1] (A version of a) Coca-Cola recipe.

13.5 kg (30 lb) sugar
7.5 l (2 gallons) water
1 l (1 quart) lime juice
120 g (4 oz) citrate of caffeine
60 g (2 oz) citric acid
30 ml (1 oz) vanilla extract

22 ml (¾ oz) fluid extract of kola
22 ml (¾ oz) fluid extract of coca

Combine the extracts and set aside. Dissolve the lime juice, caffeine and citric acid in 1 l (1 quart) of water and set aside. Dissolve the sugar in the remainder of the water over a gentle heat to make a syrup. When it is cool, add the other two solutions and mix thoroughly. Colour with caramel.

OpenCola

This is an 'open-source' cola, created as a response to the secret recipes of Coca-Cola and Pepsi, as it appears on Wikipedia. Makers are invited to create and modify this recipe. This is obviously not for children, beginners or anyone with other things to do, but the ingredients and steps demonstrate how complicated cola is. Like many modern colas, it doesn't have kola nut or coca in it.

For the flavouring:
3.5 ml (¾ tsp) orange oil
1 ml (¼ tsp) lemon oil
1 ml (¼ tsp) nutmeg oil
1.25 ml (¼ tsp) cassia (cinnamon) oil
0.25 ml (¹⁄₂₀ tsp) coriander oil
0.25 ml (¹⁄₂₀ tsp) neroli oil (similar to petitgrain,
bergamot or bitter orange oil)
2.75 ml (½ tsp) lime oil
0.25 ml (¹⁄₂₀ tsp) lavender oil
10 g (⅓ oz) food-grade (not art-grade) gum arabic (thickener)
(optional)
3 ml (⅔ tsp) water

Mix the oils together. Add gum arabic and mix. Add water and mix thoroughly with a hand-mixer or blender.

The flavouring can be made in advance and stored for use later. Place in a sealed glass jar in the refrigerator, or keep at room temperature. When stored, the oils and water will separate. Just mix again before use. If used, the gum arabic will keep things together (you may need to blend the syrup to break up the gum).

For the cola:
10 ml flavouring (approximately 2 tsp packed)
3 tsp 75 per cent powder citric acid or phosphoric acid
2.3 l (80 fl. oz) water
2.4 kg (5 lb 3 oz) granulated white sugar (or equivalent sweetener)
½ tsp caffeine
30 ml (2 tbsp) caramel colour

First, make the acid solution from powder: measure 13 g (½ oz) of the acid powder and place in a small glass jar. Boil a small amount of water (or microwave 10–20 ml/2–4 teaspoons water for about a minute). Add 1 teaspoon of hot water to the powdered acid (enough to bring the total weight up to 17.5 g). Swirl the solution carefully until the powder is dissolved.

A larger batch can be made for future use, or just what is needed; 75 per cent of the total weight should be powder and 25 per cent water.

Next make the concentrate: mix 10 ml of flavouring (2 packed tsp) with the phosphoric or citric acid. Mix the water and sugar and, while mixing, add caffeine, if desired.

If your flavouring is solid (gum), it may be necessary to put some of the water into a blender, add the flavouring and acid, blend, and then add sugar and additional water to finish. Make sure the caffeine is dissolved before moving on to the next step.

Pour the acid and flavouring mixture slowly into the water/sugar mixture. Adding acid to water reduces the risk of acid splashes, as opposed to the other way around. Add caramel colour and mix. Any desired colouring can be used, or it can be left in its natural state. The colouring should not affect the taste.

Finally, make the soda: mix one part concentrate with five parts water. In other words, however much you use of the concentrate, use five times as much water. Carbonate the beverage. There are a few ways this can be accomplished: carbonate the beverage yourself, mixing soda water directly with the concentrate, instead of water in the previous step, or use a soda fountain that will combine the concentrate with carbonated water at the tap.

- Caffeine can be toxic in high doses. Be careful not to add too much to your mixture. To be safe, keep the concentration below 100 mg or 1 cup.
- Gum arabic is available in two forms: art grade and food grade. Be sure to get food-grade gum arabic; art-grade gum is toxic.
- Phosphoric acid will burn you if it touches you. If you do get acid on you, flush the affected area with water for at least 15 minutes and get medical attention.
- Many of the oils needed for flavouring can irritate skin. Use caution when preparing. They can also dissolve the plastic lining of a refrigerator. Store them in a glass container.

Cooking with Fizzy Drinks

Brisket with Coca-Cola

This is a version of a recipe that appears in various parts of the United States. Some people know it as a Southern dish, but it is also a traditional dish at the Jewish holiday of Passover.

2 tbsp packed light brown sugar
1 tbsp salt
1 tbsp sweet paprika
2 tsp onion powder
1 tsp ground black pepper
2 kg (4 lb) beef brisket, trimmed
2 tbsp vegetable oil

4 onions, thinly sliced
3 carrots, thickly sliced
470 ml (2 cups) cola
800 ml (28 oz) can crushed tomatoes

Combine brown sugar, salt, paprika, onion powder and pepper in a small bowl. Rub mixture all over meat, cover in cling film, and refrigerate overnight.

Preheat the oven to 170°/150°C fan (325°F). Heat the vegetable oil in a large Dutch oven over medium-high heat. Place the brisket into the pot, fat side down, and sear the meat until richly browned, about 6 minutes per side. Transfer to a plate.

Add the sliced onions to the oil left in the pot and cook until softened, about 12 to 15 minutes. Keep the pot covered and stir frequently to prevent burning. Add the carrots, cover, and cook, stirring until softened, about 5 more minutes. Transfer onions and carrots to a bowl.

Deglaze the pan by adding Coca-Cola and tomatoes. Scrape the bottom of the pot with the back of a wooden spoon to dissolve all of the brown caramelized bits.

Place the brisket into the Dutch oven along with any juices. Place the carrots and onions around the meat. If needed, add enough water to keep the meat half-submerged in liquid. Cover the pot tightly with aluminium foil before closing the lid. Place in the oven to braise slowly for 3 hours.

Gently remove the brisket from its braising liquid and allow it to rest on a board, tented with aluminium foil, for 30 minutes. Raise the oven temperature to 200°C/425°F.

Slice the rested meat across the grain into 6-cm (2¼-in.) slices. Spoon off any accumulated fat from the top of the juices left in the Dutch oven and return the sliced brisket to the pot.

Return the pot to the oven, uncovered, and cook until the meat is fork-tender, about 30 to 40 minutes. Remove the pot from the oven and let stand for 15 minutes before removing the sliced brisket to a platter. Spoon over the onions, carrots and sauce, and serve immediately.

Irn-Bru Cupcakes

For the cupcakes;
125 g (4½ oz) plain flour, sieved
125 g (4½ oz) caster sugar
¼ tsp bicarbonate of soda
½ tsp baking powder
¼ tsp salt
125 ml (4½ fl. oz) buttermilk
½ tsp vanilla extract
125 g (4½ oz) unsalted butter
85 ml (3 fl. oz) Irn-Bru

Heat oven to 180°C (350°F)/160°C fan/gas mark 4. Mix the flour, sugar, bicarbonate of soda, baking powder and salt in a big bowl. Melt the butter and Irn-Bru in a pan, just until the butter melts, and remove from stove. Beat the egg and vanilla extract into buttermilk in a separate bowl. Combine buttermilk mixture with dry ingredients, mixing with spoon. Add butter/Irn-Bru, mixing with a spoon.

Divide into cupcake tins that have been lined with paper cases. Bake for 15 minutes. (Check them after 10: a straw inserted into a cake should come out clean.)

For the icing:
110 g (4 oz) icing sugar, sieved
50 g (1¾ oz) unsalted butter (soft, not melted)
¼ tsp vanilla extract

Mix icing sugar, butter and vanilla extract with a fork. Don't ice cupcakes until they are entirely cool.

References

Introduction

1 L. von Schneidemesser, 'Soda or Pop?', *Journal of English Linguistics*, XXIV (4 December 1996), pp. 270–87. The maps and analyses spawned by this article would be the envy of any academic; 'The Soda vs. Pop Map', *New York Times* (11 September 2008).
2 William Tapper quoted in Anne Cooper Funderburg, *Sundae Best: A History of Soda Fountains* (Bowling Green, KY, 2002), p. 30.
3 Lone Frank, *Mindfield: How Brain Science Is Changing Our World* (London, 2009).

1 On the Way to Fizzy Drinks

1 Frederick Slare, 'An Account of the Nature and Excellent Properties and Vertues [*sic*] of the Pyrmont Waters, 1717.'
2 See Douglas A. Simmons, *Schweppes: The First 200 Years* (London, 1983) for a detailed, well-illustrated history of the man and the company.
3 John Burnett, *Liquid Pleasures: A Social History of Drinks in Modern Britain* (London, 1999), p. 8.

4 Ibid., p. 110.

5 J. C. Drummond and A. Wilbraham, *The Englishman's Food: Five Centuries of English Diet* (London, 1957), p. 114. The authors include the vitamin content of small beer as well as its calories.

6 Ibid., p. 329. The nineteenth-century concerns about the use of tea are remarkably similar to those about drinking sweetened, carbonated beverages, including the worry that the new drinks will replace healthier foods and drinks.

7 Juliette Rossant, 'The World's First Soft Drinks', *Saudi Aramco World*, LVI/5 (September/October 2005), www.saudiaramcoworld.com.

8 Colin Emmins, *Soft Drinks: Their Origins and History* (Princes Risborough, Buckinghamshire, 1991).

9 This appears as an advertisement in the back of Soyer's own book, as part of an unpaginated advertisements section: Alexis Soyer, *The Modern Housewife; or, Ménagère* (London, 1849).

10 Henry Mayhew, *London Labour and the London Poor*, vol. 1 (London, 1861; repr. London and New York, 1968), pp. 186–92.

11 See Burnett, *Liquid Pleasures*, pp. 9–10, for the number of spas, and pp. 98–110, for statistics on soft-drink manufacturing in Britain.

12 J. E. Panton, *From Kitchen to Garret: Hints for Young Householders* (London, 1888), p. 25, cited in Burnett, *Liquid Pleasures*, p. 101.

2 Health and Pleasure: Soda Fountains

1 Anne Cooper Funderburg, *Sundae Best: A History of Soda Fountains* (Bowling Green, KY, 2002), p. 10.

2 Tristan Donovan, *Fizz: How Soda Shook Up the World* (Chicago, IL, 2014), p. 19.

3 Robert Southey, 1812, and Frederick Marryat, 1837, cited in Andrew Barr, *Drink: A Social History of America* (New York, 1995).

4 Translation of unnamed French newspaper cited in John
   H. Snively, 'Soda-water: What It Is and How It's Made',
   Harper's New Monthly Magazine, XLV/265 (August 1872), p. 345.
5 Funderburg, *Sundae Best*, pp. 27–8.
6 Mary Gay Humphreys, 'The Evolution of the Soda
   Fountain', *Harper's Weekly*, XXXV (21 November 1891), p. 923.
7 *Matthews Catalogue and Price List of Apparatus, Materials, and
   Accessories for Making and Dispensing Carbonated Beverages*
   (New York, 1891).
8 Carl J. Palmer, *History of the Soda Fountain* (Soda
   Manufacturers Association, 1947), p. 12.
9 Darcy O'Neil, *Fix the Pumps* (London, Ontario, 2009).
   O'Neil also has a website and sells phosphate for soda
   and cocktail making.
10 Constance Hays, *The Real Thing: Truth and Power at the
   Coca-Cola Company* (New York, 2004), p. 100.
11 O'Neil, *Fix the Pumps*, p. 9.
12 James Mew and John Ashton, *Drinks of the World*
   (London, 1892).
13 Funderburg, *Sundae Best*, p. 35.
14 Debra Slone, personal communication, 14 November 2019.
15 Ray Oldenburg, *The Great Good Place: Cafés, Coffee Shops,
   Community Centers, Beauty Parlors, General Stores, Bars, Hangouts,
   and How They Get You Through The Day* (New York, 1989).
16 John Somerset, 'Drug Topics', June 1921, cited in Tristan
   Donovan, *Fizz: How Soda Shook Up the World* (Chicago, IL,
   2014), p. 91.

3 Around the World in a Soda Bottle

1 Jack Brooks, 'Fountains Gain Ground in England', in
   The Soda Fountain (November 1921).
2 Douglas A. Simmons, *Schweppes: The First 200 Years*
   (London, 1983).
3 Charles Herman Sulz, *A Treatise on Beverages; or,
   The Complete Practical Bottler* (New York, 1888).

4 Big Soda

1 Émile Zola endorsement of Vin Mariani, as it appeared on the advertisements.

2 Frederick Allen, *Secret Formula: How Brilliant Marketing and Relentless Salesmanship Made Coca-Cola the Best-known Product in the World* (New York, 2000), pp. 26–8.

3 Mark Pendergrast, *For God, Country and Coca-Cola: The Unauthorized History of the Great American Soft Drink and the Company that Makes It* (New York, 2013), p. 65.

4 Ibid., p. 88.

5 Ibid.

6 Ibid.

7 Ibid., p. 463.

8 Cited in Allen, *Secret Formula*, pp. 123–4.

9 Mark Weiner, 'Consumer Culture and Participatory Democracy: The Story of Coca-Cola during World War ii', in *Food in the usa: A Reader*, ed. Carole Counihan (New York, 2002), pp. 123–41; Pendergrast, *For God, Country and Coca-Cola*, pp. 195–226; Allen, *Secret Formula*, pp. 245–78.

10 Colin Emmins, *Soft Drinks: Their Origins and History* (Princes Risborough, Buckinghamshire, 1991).

11 See Pendergrast, *For God, Country and Coca-Cola*, p. 195.

12 Ibid., p. 212.

13 Ibid.

14 Ibid., p. 211.

15 Ibid., p. 278.

16 John Burnett, *Liquid Pleasures: A Social History of Drinks in Modern Britain* (London, 1999), p. 2.

17 Pendergrast, *For God, Country and Coca-Cola*, p. 367.

5 The War(s) Against Soda

1 Marion Nestle, *Soda Politics: Taking on Big Soda (and Winning)* (New York, 2015), p. 201, quotes a Coca-Cola executive: 'the nearest thing to capitalism in a bottle'.

2 Frederick Allen, *Secret Formula: How Brilliant Marketing and Relentless Salesmanship Made Coca-Cola the Best-known Product in the World* (New York, 2000), p. 227 quotes newspaper editor William Allen White in 1938: 'The sublimated essence of all that America stands for, a decent thing, honestly made'.

3 John Burnett, *Liquid Pleasures: A Social History of Drinks in Modern Britain* (London, 1999), p. 4: 'Drink can be viewed as a factor in cementing the construction of identity as well as a means of bonding social networks.'

4 Mark Twain, in *The Tramp Abroad* (1880), writes of America's ice-water addiction, cited in Darcy O'Neil, *Fix the Pumps* (London, Ontario, 2009), p. 28.

5 An 1894 article in the *Chicago Herald* on ice-water addicts, cited ibid., p. 28; Anne Cooper Funderburg, *Sundae Best: A History of Soda Fountains* (Bowling Green, KY, 2002), p. 14.

6 On cultural attitudes to burping: 'Grepts = the sound one makes when belching after a seltzer water; the eternal sound of relief', in Vincent Brook, 'You Should See Yourself: Jewish Identity in Postmodern American Culture', in *Encyclopedia of Jewish Food*, ed. Gil Marx (Hoboken, NJ, 2010).

7 Mark Thomas, *Belching Out the Devil: Global Adventures with Coca-Cola* (New York, 2009), pp. 298–9.

8 Robert J. Foster, *Coca-globalization: Following Soft Drinks from New York to New Guinea* (New York, 2008), p. 20: Coke and Pepsi replace communion wine.

9 On objections to carbonations and burping: ibid., p. 27: association of burps with beer; Joaquina Mimoso Fachada, 'When a Local Competitor (Slightly) Shakes Up the Global Giants: A Case on the Soft Drink Market', MA thesis, Escola de Administração de Empresas de São Paolo, 2011.

10 *Westport Times* (New Zealand), citing a story from the *Detroit [Michigan] Free Press*, x/1358, p. 4. It is a humorous anecdote about a man who works at a soda fountain teasing a woman customer with no claim that it is a true story.

11 Sidney Mintz, *Sweetness and Power: The Place of Sugar in Modern History* (New York, 1985).

12 Michael F. Jacobson, *Liquid Candy: How Soft Drinks are Harming Americans' Health, Center for Science in the Public Interest*, 2nd edn (Washington, DC, 2005).

13 For example, Mark Thomas, *Belching Out the Devil: Global Adventures with Coca-Cola* (New York, 2009)

14 For a useful and concise history of artificial sweeteners in soft drinks (and disputes about those sweeteners), see Tristan Donovan, *Fizz: How Soda Shook Up the World* (Chicago, IL, 2014), pp. 169–76.

15 A. Mullee et al., 'Association Between Soft Drink Consumption and Mortality in 10 European Countries', *JAMA Internal Medicine* (3 September 2019).

16 Constance L. Hays, *The Real Thing: Truth and Power at the Coca-Cola Company* (New York, 2004), p. 265.

17 For example, Gary Alan Fine, 'The Kentucky Fried Rat: Legends and Modern Society', *Journal of the American Folklore Institute*, CXVII/2–3 (May–December 1980), pp. 222–43. Fine argues that modern legends, including those about mice in Coca-Cola bottles or rats at a Kentucky Fried Chicken chain, are a response, in part, to distrust of large, impersonal corporations.

18 Regarding contaminants in Coca-Cola in Brussels and India, as well as labour disputes, the use of child labour, the depletion of ground water and other abuses of people and the earth, see Thomas, *Belching Out the Devil*; Bartow J. Elmore, *Citizen Coke: The Making of Coca-Cola Capitalism* (New York, 2014); Michael Blanding, *The Coke Machine: The Dirty Truth behind the World's Favorite Soft Drink* (New York, 2010).

19 Tom Standish, *A History of the World in 6 Glasses* (New York, 2006), pp. 257–8.

20 Dorothy Hartley, *Food in England* (London, 1954; revd edn, 1985), p. 537.

21 Chitrita Banerji, *Eating India: An Odyssey into the Food and Culture of the Land of Spices* (New York and London, 2007), p. 163.

22 Mintz, *Sweetness and Power*.

23 Foster, *Coca-globalization*, p. 3.

24 Peter Heine, *Food Culture in the Near East, Middle East, and North Africa* (Westport, CT, 2004), p. 69.

25 On 'anti-Cokes', see, for instance, Foster, *Coca-globalization*, pp. 173–7.

26 'Sugar-sweetened Beverages and Sugar Taxes: An Overview, Index and Resource Guide', Hunter College NYC Food Policy Center, 5 February 2020, https://nycfoodpolicy.org. The website for the Center contains excellent resources and websites.

27 Anna H. Grummon, Benjamin B. Lockwood, Dmitry Taubinsky and Hunt Allcott, 'Designing Better Sugary Drink Taxes', *Science*, CCCLV/6457 (September 2019), pp. 989–90.

6 Plus ça Change

1 Robert J. Foster, *Coca-globalization: Following Soft Drinks from New York to New Guinea* (New York, 2008), pp. 68–9.

2 Seth Stevenson, 'I'd Like to Buy the World a Shelf-stable Children's Lactic Drink', *New York Times Magazine* (10 March 2002), www.nytimes.com.

3 Bill McKibben, *Deep Economy: The Wealth of Communities and the Durable Future* (New York, 2007).

4 Siobhan Downes, 'How This British Soft Drink Became a Ramadan Classic', 9 May 2019, www.whatson.ae.

5 John Nese (owner of soda retailer Galco), personal communication, telephone, 12 June 2016.

6 Tim Richardson, 'Coke Freestyle vs. Pepsi Spire: The Cola Wars Re-ignite!', www.enlivenllc.com, 10 May 2016.

7 James Mew and John Ashton, *Drinks of the World* (1892).

Recipes

1 See Layla Eplett, 'I'd Like to Make the World A Coke: Attempting the "Original" Coca-Cola Formula', *Scientific American*, 27 July 2015, https://blogs.scientificamerican.com.

Select Bibliography

Allen, Frederick, *Secret Formula: How Brilliant Marketing
    and Relentless Salesmanship Made Coca-Cola the Best-known
    Product in the World* (New York, 2000)
Banerji, Chitrita, *Eating India: An Odyssey into the Food and
    Culture of the Land of Spices* (New York and London, 2007)
Barber, Benjamin R., *Consumed* (London, 2007)
Barr, Andrew, *Drink: A Social History of America*
    (New York, 1995)
Blanding, Michael, *The Coke Machine: The Dirty Truth
    behind the World's Favorite Soft Drink* (London and
    New York, 2010)
Burnett, John, *Liquid Pleasures: A Social History of Drinks
    in Modern Britain* (London, 1999)
Donovan, Tristan, *Fizz: How Soda Shook Up the World*
    (Chicago, IL, 2014)
Drummond, J. C. and Wilbraham A., *The Englishman's Food:
    Five Centuries of English Diet* (London, 1957)
Elmore, Bartow J., *Citizen Coke: The Making of Coca-Cola
    Capitalism* (New York, 2014)
Emerson, Edward R., *Beverages, Past and Present* (New York, 1908)
Emmins, Colin, *Soft Drinks: Their Origins and History* (Princes
    Risborough, Buckinghamshire, 1991)
—, 'Soft Drinks', in *Cambridge World History of Food*,
    ed. Kenneth F. Kipple and Kriemhild Connee Ornelas
    (Cambridge, 2001), vol. 1, pp. 702–12

Foster, Robert J., *Coca-Globalization: Following Soft Drinks from New York to New Guinea* (New York, 2008)

Frank, Lone, *Mindfield: How Brain Science Is Changing Our World* (London, 2009)

Funderburg, Anne Cooper, *Sundae Best: A History of Soda Fountains* (Bowling Green, KY, 2002)

Giasullo, Gia, Peter Freeman and Elizabeth Kiem, *The Soda Fountain: Floats, Sundaes, Egg Creams, and More – Stories and Flavors of an American Original* (New York, 2014)

Hartley, Dorothy, *Food in England* (London, 1954)

Hays, Constance L., *The Real Thing: Truth and Power at the Coca-Cola Company* (New York, 2004)

Heine, Peter, *Food Culture in the Near East, Middle East, and North Africa* (Westport, CT, 2004)

Humphreys, Mary Gay, 'The Evolution of the Soda Fountain', *Harper's Weekly*, XXXV (21 November 1891), pp. 923–4

Lears, Jackson, *Fables of Abundance: A Cultural History of Advertising in America* (New York, 1994)

Louis, J. C., and Harvey Z. Yazijian, *The Cola Wars: The Story of the Global Corporate Battle Between the Coca-Cola Company and PepsiCo, Inc.* (New York, 1980)

McCann, Mac, 'Sippin' and Spittin': Examining the Use of Lean in Hip-hop', 6 May 2014, https://macmccanntx.com

The Matthews Catalogue and Price List of Apparatus, Materials, and Accessories for Making and Dispensing Carbonated Beverages (New York, 1891)

Mayhew, Henry, *London Labour and the London Poor* (London, 1861; repr. London and New York, 1968), vol. I

Mew, James, and John Ashton, *Drinks of the World* (London and New York, 1892)

Martin, Milward W., *Twelve Full Ounces*, 2nd edn (New York, 1969)

Mimoso Fachada, Joaquina, 'When a Local Competitor (Slightly) Shakes Up the Global Giants: A Case on the Soft Drink Market', dissertation (Escola de Administração de Empresas de São Paolo, 2011)

Mintz, Sidney, *Sweetness and Power: The Place of Sugar in Modern History* (New York, 1985)

Nestle, Marion, *Soda Politics: Taking on Big Soda (and Winning)* (New York, 2015)

Oldenburg, Ray, *The Great Good Place: Cafés, Coffee Shops, Community Centers, Beauty Parlors, General Stores, Bars, Hangouts, and How They Get You through the Day* (New York, 1989)

O'Neil, Darcy S., *Fix the Pumps: The History and Recipes of the Soda Fountain* (London, Ontario, 2009)

Pendergrast, Mark, *For God, Country and Coca-Cola: The Unauthorized History of the Great American Soft Drink and the Company that Makes It* (New York, 2013)

Riley, John J., *A History of the American Soft Drink Industry: Bottled Carbonated Beverages, 1807–1957* (Washington, DC, 1958)

Rossant, Juliette. 'The World's First Soft Drink', *Saudi Aramco World*, LVI/5 (September/October 2005), www.saudiaramcoworld.com

Schneidemesser, L. 'Soda or Pop?', *Journal of English Linguistics*, IV/24 (December 1996), pp. 270–87

Simmons, Douglas A., *Schweppes: The First 200 Years* (London, 1983)

Smith, Andrew F., *Drinking History: Fifteen Turning Points in the Making of American Beverages* (New York, 2012)

Snively, John H., 'Soda-water: What It Is and How It's Made', *Harper's New Monthly Magazine*, XLV/265 (August 1872), pp. 341–6

'The Soda vs. Pop Map', *New York Times* (11 September 2008)

Soyer, Alexis, *The Modern Housewife; or, Ménagère* (London, 1849)

Standish, Tom, *A History of the World in 6 Glasses* (New York, 2006)

Stevenson, Seth, 'I'd Like to Buy the World a Shelf-stable Children's Lactic Drink', *New York Times Magazine* (10 March 2002), www.nytimes.com

Sulz, Charles Herman, *A Treatise on Beverages; or, The Complete Practical Bottler* (New York, 1888)

Thomas, Mark, *Belching Out the Devil: Global Adventures with Coca-Cola* (New York, 2009)

Weiner, Mark, 'Consumer Culture and Participatory Democracy: The Story of Coca-Cola During World War II', in *Food in the U.S.A.: A Reader*, ed. Carole Counihan (New York, 2002), pp. 123–41

Young Witzel, Gyvel, and Michael Karl Witzel, *Soda Pop! From Miracle Medicine to Pop Culture* (Stillwood, MN, 1998)

Websites and Associations

Drink Tasting and Fun

www.artofdrink.com

http://colatest.com (in German and some English)

www.delicioussparklingtemperancedrinks.net

www.dizzyfrinks.com

www.drugstoremuseum.com
(virtual soda fountain museum)

https://exoticpop.com

https://fivestarsoda.com (craft soda tastings)

www.kolakult.de (German)

https://raredrank.com
(Canadian seller of unusual drinks to U.S.)

https://sodafinder.com

The-Soft-Drinks.com

Action against Sugary Drinks

www.actiononsugar.org

www.cspinet.org (Center for Science in the Public Interest)

International Industry Sites

www.britishsoftdrinks.com

www.coca-cola.com

www.euromonitor.com (mostly sells reports but also has information about the international drinks business)

Acknowledgements

Any book that takes this long to write leaves the author grateful to more people than she can remember to thank, not the least being Michael Leaman, Amy Salter and Alexandru Ciobanu at Reaktion Books, and Andrew Smith, editor of the Edible Series.

I was helped through this process by the denizens of the educator's breakroom of Lower East Side Tenement Museum and by other members of the museum's education department, who tasted fizzy drinks with me and told me stories of soda in the places they were born, lived or travelled. They shared their experiences of growing up with Inca Kola or of first encountering Western soda or of missing the flavours of drinks of their childhood. They told me about regional carbonated drinks I had never heard of and would certainly not have known to ask about. In all these ways, they brought alive for me what I was reading and writing about and reminded me of the importance of the sweet, fizzy stuff.

I thank the friends who told me of what soda meant in rural Egypt (Dwight Reynolds), and in Japan just after the Second World War (Jiro Yamada), and in modern Bali (Laurie Pollock). This is going to be an incomplete list, no matter what I do. Thank you, all.

People at a variety of institutions have patiently answered questions and sent artwork, including John Nese at Galco; Liz Sherman, director of the New Orleans Pharmacy Museum; Pavia Burroughs at the Franklin Fountain in Philadelphia; J Del Conner of Dr. Physick Soda; and, especially, the historian of the Zaharakos Ice Cream Parlor and Museum, Debra Slone.

I want to thank my family, including the granddaughters to whom this book is dedicated: Emily, who called soda 'tingly' as a small child and, as a teen, told me about Starbucks as a soda fountain, and Nicole, who has an excellent palate for soda tasting and a natural ability to describe the way Ramune tastes different from American sodas. Special thanks go to my cousin Rob Brill for his editorial help.

My partner, Laura Melano Flanagan, has been patient (most of the time) and loving (all of the time) for the years it took to write this book, and many more years than that, and I am grateful beyond words for her presence in my life.

Photo Acknowledgements

The author and publishers wish to express their thanks to the below sources of illustrative material and/or permission to reproduce it. Some locations of artworks are also given below, in the interest of brevity:

Collection of the author: pp. 30, 33, 78; from Louis Figuier, *Les merveilles de l'industrie, ou Description des principales industries modernes*, vol. III (Paris, 1873–7): p. 13; Sheila Fitzgerald/Shutterstock.com: p. 71; photo courtesy The Franklin Fountain, Philadelphia, PA: p. 139; Heritage Auctions, Ha.com: pp. 82, 83; photo Patrick Hofrichter/Pexels: p. 6; The J. Paul Getty Museum, Los Angeles: p. 49; photo Judd Joffre/Judd's Memphis Kitchen: p. 8; photo Mark Kauffman/The LIFE Picture Collection via Getty Images: p. 108; Tetiana Kolubai/iStock.com: p. 67; photos Judith Levin: pp. 133, 134; Library of Congress, Prints and Photographs Division, Washington, DC: pp. 28, 58, 60; courtesy Missouri Historical Society, St Louis: p. 55; The Museum of Modern Art, Ibaraki: p. 72; National Archives at College Park, MD: p. 92; New-York Historical Society: p. 41; The New York Public Library: p. 32; from Orrin Chalfant Painter, *William Painter and His Father, Dr Edward Painter* (Baltimore, MD, 1914), photo Allen County Public Library, Fort Wayne, IN: p. 68; from Joseph Priestley, *Directions for Impregnating Water with Fixed Air* (London, 1772), photo Wellcome Library, London: p. 19; Rijksmuseum, Amsterdam: p. 17; from Adolphe Smith, *Street Life in London* (London, 1877), photo LSE Library

Index

italic numbers refer to illustrations; **bold** to recipes

7-Up (drink, U.S.) 79, 101
815 Cola (drink, South Korea)
      111

acid phosphate 51
Adkins, William S 52, 53
advertising and marketing 12,
      13, 15, *17, 22,* 29, 32, 33–4,
      33, 36, 54, *59, 64, 65, 66,* 71,
      73, 76–7, 78–81, *80, 82, 86,*
      87, 88–9, 91, 93, 97, 104,
      101, 111, *112,* 116, 123–6,
      135, 136, 138, 140
Africa 12, 65, 84, 92, 103, 109,
      110, 111, 113,
Afri-Cola (drink, Germany)
      110
alcohol 15, 24–9, 36, 37, 53,
      57, 58, *58,* 64, 66, 68, 70,
      72, 91, 99, 100, 102, 127,
      128, 136, 137
Alderton, Charles 81
Algeria 66
Allen, Frederick 85
antiscorbutic 19, 20, 70

Arabic influences on
      European soft drinks 27
artificial sweeteners 51, 53, 97,
      105, 127
Ashton, John 53
Atlanta, Georgia 82, 85, 110
Austen, Ben 44
Australia 10, *18, 30, 62,* 63, 65,
      73, 92, 130
Austria 130
Avery (U.S. company) 124

Backer, Bill 89
Bacon, Francis 27
Balkans 65
Banerji, Chitrita 108–9
Banta (North India) 74, 135
      see also Goli Soda
Baptista de Andrade, Pedro
      66
barley water 24, 32, 37
Barr, Robert 74
Bashew, Marx and Harry 73
Berkeley, California 114
Berlin *24, 65*

Bermuda 114
Bickford, William 73
'Big Soda' 77, 79–96, 97, 118,
    119, 136
Bio Cola (UK) 113
Bionade Organic Health
    Drink (Bavaria) 118, 126–7
Birch beer 50
Black, Joseph 18
Bloomberg, Michael 91, 114
bottles and bottle stoppers 10,
    17, *18*, 65, 68, *68*, *69*, 69–70,
    71, 73, 74, 77, *80*, 90, 94–5,
    105–6, 109, 120–24, 133,
    135
    see also INDIVIDUAL BOTTLE
    TYPES
bottling 39, 65, 66, *68*, 73, *74*,
    76, 88, 89, 92, 105, 118
Boston, Massachusetts 7, 44
Bradham, Caleb 88
brands and proprietary
    products 8, 11, 13, 29, 31,
    50, 79–81, 88, 91, 113,
    124, 131, 132, 135, 136
Brazil 68, 73, 90–1, 121, 133
Breizh Cola (Breton, France)
    113
Breton Cola (Breton, France)
    100
brewing (fermentation) 18, 19,
    24, 25, 34, 68, 79, 89, 99,
    108, 127, 136
brisket with Coca-Cola **154–5**
Brown, Maynard *22*
Brussels 106
Burnett, John 23, 93–4

Bursas (brand) *30*
burping 99–100

caffeine 24, 68, 84, 85, 97,
    98–9, 104, 121, 129, 130
Calpis (also Calpico) *72*, 73, 120
Cambodia 133
Canada 61, 63, 64, 130
Canada Dry *59*, 64
Candler, Asa 85–8, 90
cans 94, 121–3, 130
Cantrell, Joseph 64, 66
carbon dioxide 18–19, *21*, 43,
    44, 48, 51, 97, 106, 137
Carbonated Soft Drinks (CSD)
    (industry category) 9
Cardomom Sparkler **147**
Central America 66
    see also INDIVIDUAL
    COUNTRIES
'Champagne' 64, 66
Cheerwine (drink, U.S.) 132
China 11, 111, 133
China Cola (U.S.), also The
    Chinese People's Own
    Cola (China) 111, 113
Church of the Latter Day
    Saints (Mormons) 128–9
cider (also cyder) 42, 50, 72
cocaine 82, 88, 94, 98
Coca-Cola 98–9, **151–2**
    advertising and marketing
    79, 81, 81, *82*, 82–3, 85, *86*,
    89, 90, 91, 92, 93, 95–6,
    98, 109, 123
    company 81, 92, *92*, 94–7,
    103, 106, 110, 116, 118, 119

early history 9, 79, 81, 82–91
Second World War *83*, 91–3
other Coca-Cola Company drinks 81, 119, 121, 135, 137
as symbolic of America or of Western values 9, 79, 91, 93, 94, 97, 100, 107, *108*, 109, 111, 113
Coca-Colonization 12, *108*
Codd bottles (Codd-neck bottles) 69–70, 74, 120, 135, *135*
Codd, Hiram 69
Cola flavour 85
Colombia 66, 135
contaminants 79, 100, 106
cordial 25, 91
Cracker Barrel Old Country Store and Restaurant 132
Cream Soda: Using Cow's Cream for Fountains **144**
Crown cork *68*, 70
Curious Elixirs (brand, u.s.) 128

dandelion and burdock 26, *30*, 132
democracy 48, 88
Denmark 107
diet soda 105, 114, 122
    see also artificial sweeteners
'dirty soda' 128–9
'Don't Care' (flavour) 53
Don't Care Syrup **145**
Dows, Gustavus 44, 45

Dr. Brown Cel-Ray (drink, u.s.) 7, *8*, 9
Dr. Chase's Recipes **143, 144**
Dr Pepper *80*, 81, 85, 100
drugstore *see* pharmacy
Drummond, JC 26
Dry Soda (brand, u.s.) 127
Dubai 124
Dubelle, G. H. **145**
Dublin Dr Pepper 132–3

East and West Indies 65
Ebert, Albert Ethelbert 52, 53
egg cream 7
Egyptienne Egg Shake **148**
Eisenhower, Dwight D. 91
exhibitions and world fairs
    Centennial Exhibition, Philadelphia (1876) *49*, 50, 80, 125
    Exposition Universelle, Paris (1867) 45
    Exposition Universelle, Paris (1878) *46*
    Great Exhibition, London (1851) 31
    World's Fair, St Louis, Missouri (1904) 55
exoticism 31, 36, 50, 117, 138

fast food (also 'junk food') 36, 60, 90, 94, 96, 103, 104, 118, 126, 137
Fentimans (company, uk) 132, *133*, 138, 138
Figuier, Louis, *Les merveilles de l'industrie 13*

Fiji 93
Food for Specified Health
      Uses (FOSHU) Japan 129
For His Son (film) 109
France 28, 46, 63, 100, 107, *108*,
      111, 113
      Paris *25*, 28, 45, 48, *108*,
      111
Franklin Fountain
      (Philadelphia) *139*, **148**
Freestyle (vending machine,
      Coca-Cola Company) 125
'functionals' *see* medicinal
      claims and beliefs
Funderburg, Anne 54
Future Cola (China) 111, 113

Gasogene 20, 36, 47, 136
Gatorade 129
Georgia (country) 64–5
Germany 15, 16, *17*, *24*, 47, 63,
      64, *65*, 110, *112*, 113
ginger (flavour) 8, 26, 27, 29,
      47, 50, 63, 127, 130
ginger ale
      dry 58, *59*, 64, 70, 73, 79
      golden 58, 64, 66, 123, 132
      unspecified 7, 31, 70, 73,
      79, 123
ginger beer *18*, *24*, 25, 26, 34–6,
      35, 42, 47, 65, 68, 121, 126,
      136, 138
Glam Cola (Germany) 127
glamour 30, 51, 54, 87, 101
Gods Must Be Crazy, The (film)
      109, *110*
Goizueta, Roberto 96

glucose-fructose syrup 95–6,
      97, 104, 116, 127, 131
      see also high-fructose corn
      syrup
Goli soda (South India) 74,
      135
Green River (drink, U.S.) 132
guarana fruit 66, 68
guarana sodas 66, 68, 73, 90,
      121, 129, 133,
GuS Grown-up Soda (brand,
      U.S.) 127
Guy, Francis, *Tontine Coffee
      House 41*

Hamilton bottles (torpedo
      bottles) *18*, 69
Hamoud Boualem (brand,
      Algeria) 66
Hangzhou Wahaha (company)
      China 111–12
Hankow Er Chang (brand,
      China) 133–4
Hartley, Dorothy 107–8
Hawkins, Joseph 41
health concerns 30, 97
      addiction 97–8, 102, 107
      artificial sweeteners 51,
      97, 105
      caffeine 97, 98, 127
      carcinogens 105
      carbon dioxide 11, 17,
      19, 43, 51, 97, 106, 137
      contamination 23, 97, 100,
      102, 105
      E numbers/artificial
      flavours or colours 53, 97

ice/cold drinks 11, 23, 27, 97–8
obesity 103–4, 113
phosphoric acid 90, 97, 100, 106, 127
sugar 7, 96, 102–5, 113–15, *115*, 130, 131
Helmont, Jon Baptista van 18
Henry, Thomas, 21
herbal medicine 128, 130
high-fructose corn syrup 95–6, 97, 104, 116, 127, 131
see also glucose-fructose syrup
Hires, Charles E. 79
Hires Root Beer *78*, 79, 98, 100
Hiss, A. Emil 53, **145**
Holmes Jr, Oliver Wendell 90
'hot soda' 52, 123, 137
Hutchinson bottles and stoppers *69*, 70
Hunter, John 119

Iceland 134
Iftar 76, 77, 111
Inca Kola (drink, Peru) 73, 74, *79*, 135
India 76, 106, 108, 121, 123, 135
Indian Paneer Soda **149**
Iran 12, 111
Ireland 10, 18, 41, 63, 64, 113
Irn-Bru (drink, Scotland) 79, 100, 114, 118

Irn-Bru Cupcakes **156**
Italy 27, 52, 57, 63, 107, 109, 136

Japan 11, 70–72, 119–21, 123, 124, 129, 136
Jamaica 65
Jefferson, Thomas 16
Jenks, William J. 43
Jewish 7, 52, *64*, 99
Jones Soda Co. 124, *125*, 126
Julmust (drink, Sweden) 68

Kia-Ora (UK) 121
kola nut 84, *84*, 85
Kola Champagne 66
Kola Román (Columbia) 135
kombucha 136
Kroc, Ray 94
kumis 73
Kuwait 124
kvass (drink, Russia) 136, **150–51**

Ladd, J. *18*
Lagidze waters *67*
Laranjada 66
Lava Cola (Vanuatu) 130
lawsuits 88, 90, 100, 106, 133
'lean' 122
lemonade 26, 28, 32, 35, 36, 37, 42, 63, 64, 65, 66, *67*, 70, 73, 79, 109, 132, 135
limonadiers 28
Lindley, José Robinson 73
Lippincott, Charles *49*, 50, 80
Liquid Carbonic 55, *55*
liquorice water 24, *25*

lithium 101
London 16, *18*, *20*, 21, 23, 26, 27, 31–7, 63, 69, 100, 103, 138
Lorina (drink, French) 66
Luyken, Jan, *Bathhouse Aacchen* *17*

McArthur, Douglas 91
McBride, David 18
McDonald's 77, 118
McKibben, Bill 124
McLaughlin, John 64
Maltextrakt (Iceland) *134*
Manchester, England 74
Mariani, Angelo 82
marijuana 130
Marryat, Frederick 42, 48
'Mary Jane's Relaxing Soda' (drink, U.S.) 130
Mathlouthi, Tawfik 111
Matthews, John 44, 47, *47*, 48, 50, 54
Maya 99, 109, 110
Mayhew, Henry 34–6, 100
Mecca Cola 12, 111
medicinal claims and beliefs 9, 15, 17, 29–31, *30*, 42, 59, 73, 80, 82, 103, 128, 129, 130
memories and associations 9, 12, 13, 59, 71, 76, 77, 81 91, 92, 100, 111, 117, 118, 122, 132 137, 138
Mew, James **53**
Mexico 99, 103, 113, 114
Middle East 75, 111

Miller and Shoemaker's Corner Pharmacy 39
mineral water(s) 12, 15, 16–17, 23, 32, 39, 40–42, 47 50, 65, 68
Mintz, Sidney 109
Mint Kvass **150–51**
Mitrofane Lagidze (brand) *67*
More-or-less-Japanese Homemade Melon Soda **149–50**
'mouthfeel' 51
Moxie (drink, U.S.) 86, 132
Muslims, drink traditions of 27, 75, 76, 111, 128

Nakamura Tsune, *Still-life with Calpis Wrapping Paper 72*
Native peoples 16, 30
nectar 26–7, 32, 33–4, 36, 42, *47*, 52, **147–8**
Nese, John Galco's Soda Pop Shop 126, 135–6
New Haven, Connecticut 40
New Orleans Nectar Soda **147–8**
New York City 40–42, *41*, 44, 48, 52, 63, *64*, 65, 95, 101, 114, 133
Nichols, John Joel 74
Nooth, John 20, *20*
Nooth's apparatus 43
Nooyi, Indra 137
Not Your Father's Root Beer (brand, U.S.) 136

novelty 37, 51, 52, 117, 119,
    120, 122, 123, 124–5, 126,
    126, *128*, 131, 137, 138 140
    see also exoticism

obesity *see* health concerns
Oldenburg, Ray 57
Open Cola **151–4**

Painter, William *68*, 70
Pakistan 123
Palin, Sarah *95*
Papua New Guinea 93, 99
Parsi Cola (Middle East) 111
Påskmust (drink, Sweden) 68
patent medicines 15, 29–31,
    82, 84, 86, 129
Patton, George 91
Pemberton, John S 82–5
Pendergrast, Mark 89
Pepsi-Cola 87, 88, 89, 94–5,
    99, 111, 121
    novelty flavours 119, 121
PepsiCo 89, 106–7, 119,
    122, 125, 137
Pepys, Samuel 23
Perry, Matthew 70
Persian Sherbet **143**
Peru 73, *74*, 79, 82, 113, 135
pharmacy 15, 38, 39, 40, 43,
    44, 57, 70, 73, 138
Philadelphia 40, 41, 43, 49,
    49, 50, 79, 80, 114, 125,
    138, *139*, 171
phosphoric acid 52, 85,
    90, 97, 100, 106, 127
    see also health concerns

Physick, Philip Sung 138
Pocari Sweat (drink, Japan)
    120, 129
'Pop v Soda' *10*
Posh Pop (drink, UK) 126
Postobón (company,
    Columbia) 66
Priestley, Joseph 17, 19, *19*
Prohibition 50, *57*, 58, *58*,
    79, 100, 127
Puerto Rico *75*
Pure Food and Drugs Act
    (U.S.) 89, 98

Ramadan 76, 124
    see also Iftar
Ramune *71*, 71–2, 118, 120
Roberts, Harry and Robert
    68
Robinson, Frank 85
Rocket Fizz (company) 126
Rockwell, Norman 59
Roosevelt, Franklin 91
root beer 25, 26, 50, 64, *78*,
    78–81, 98, 100, 136
Root-beer Essence: Ottawa or
    Otaki Root Beer **144–5**
Rosemary Plum Soda **148–9**
Royal Crown (RC) Cola *87*, 88
Russia 11, 65

Salt Lake City, Utah 128
San Pellegrino (brand) 114
sarsaparilla 26, *30*, 32, 50, 64,
    73
sassafras 26
Saudi Arabia 75, 76

Schweppe, Jacob (also Jacob
    Schweppe and Company)
    18, 21, *21*
Schweppes (Company) *22*,
    23, 31, 32, *32*, 34, 36, 47,
    65, 69
Scotland 15, 70, 79
scurvy 19, 20
Second World War, and soda
    12, 91–93, 114, 116
secret recipes 30, 74, 81, 89,
    100–101
Seltzer 7, *13*, 15, 73, 99, 136
seltzogene *20*
Senegal 84
Shariba 27
sherbet (also sherbert) 27, *28*,
    108, **143**
shrub 27, 136
Silliman, Benjamin 140–41
Sim, Alexander Cameron 70
Sinalco (brand) 64, *65*, *66*
Singapore 123
siphon 7, 13, 61, 136
Slare, Frederick 16
Slow Cow (Quebec) 130
small beers 24, 26
    kinderbier 26
Smith, Aldophe, *Street Life in
    London 35*
Snapple (company) 137
social media 123–4, 137
soda as 'American' 9, 43, 45–6,
    62, 63, 111
soda fountains (places) 7, 16,
    37, *38*, 39–60, *49*, *56*, *58*, *60*,
    61, *62*, 63, 64, 70, 79, 80,

85, *86*, 86, 89, 90, 94, 100,
    101, 121, 123, 129, 136,
    137, 138, *139*
soda fountains (equipment)
    39 60, *45*, *47*, *49*, *56*, 61,
    63, 125
soda and sugary drinks taxes
    90, 113–16, *115*, 121, 136
SodaStream 136
Soda sữa hột gà (Vietnam and
    Cambodia) 133, **151**
soft drinks
    relationship to alcoholic
    drinks 15, 25–6, 57, 127–9,
    136
    traditional, historical or
    regional (not fizzy) 23, 24,
    27–28, 108–9, 127
Soft Drinks Industry (War
    Time) Association (UK) 91
Soft Drinks Industry Levy
    (UK) 114
South Africa 65, 73, *110*
South America 10, 61, 66, 99
    see also INDIVIDUAL
    COUNTRIES
Southey, Robert 42
Soyer, Alexis 32, 33, 36
Spain 63
Speakerman, Townsend 40
Spire (PepsiCo, vending
    machine) 125, 137
sports drinks 120, 129, 130
Sprite (drink, U.S.) 111, 121
spruce beer *25*
squash 25
Starbucks 138

Stock Champagne Syrup **145**

Stoney Tangawizi (drink, Africa)

Sultz, Charles Herman 70, **144**

Super Big Gulp (7-Eleven, U.S.) 95

Sweden 68, 123

switchel 27, 136

syrup 27

tea 11, 23, 24, 26–7, 52, 60, 94, 96, 103, 114, 119, 121, 127, 130, 136, 137

'Technical observers' 92, *92*

temperance 47, 57–8, 74, 80, 98, 127

Thailand 130

Thomas, Mark Belching 140

Thompson, John *35*

Thompson, William Tappan 11

Thums Up (cola, India) 121, 135

tonic (quinine water) 7

tonics, health (including 'brain tonics') 7, 15, *30*, 73, 74, 81, 82–3, 88, *101*, 130, 140

see also medicinal claims and beliefs

Tontine Coffee House 40, *41*

TÖST (drink, U.S.) 127

Tufts, James W. *45*, 50, 80, 125

Turka Cola 97, 111

Turkey *28*, 111

Ubuntu Cola 113

Usher, George 41

vending machines 83, 120, 125, 125, 137

Vernor's Ginger Ale (drink, U.S.) 132

Very Nice Lemon Syrup, A **144**

Vienna, Austria 107

Vietnam 133

Vimto 74, *76*, 91, 100, 111, 124, 137

Vin Mariani (alcoholic drink, French) 82

Vita-Cola (drink, East Germany) *112*

Washington, George 16

Washington (U.S. state) 114

Wiley, Harvey Washington 98–9

Women's Christian Temperance Union (WCTU) 98

Woodruff, Robert 90, 91

Woolton, Lord (Frederick Marquis) 91

World Health Organization (WHO) 103–4, 113

World's Fair Fruit Champagne **145–6**

Zaharakos (family name, soda fountain, U.S.) 54–56, *56*

ZamZam (cola, Iran) 111